WALKING
THE
INDIAN
STREETS

OTHER BOOKS BY VED MEHTA

Face to Face
Fly and the Fly-Bottle
The New Theologian
Delinquent Chacha
Portrait of India
John Is Easy to Please

WALKING THE INDIAN STREETS

VED MEHTA

*Revised Edition, with a new
introduction by the author*

WEIDENFELD AND NICOLSON
5 Winsley Street London W1

First edition 1960

Revised edition 1971; first published in Great Britain 1971

Most of the material, in slightly different form,
appeared originally in *The New Yorker*.

ISBN 0 297 00374 7

Printed in Great Britain by Bristol Typesetting Co Ltd
Barton Manor - St Philips, Bristol

To Christoper Hill and R. W. Southern

I am indebted to Joan Hartman for her friendship, suggestions, and helpful and sometimes stubborn criticism, and to Harriet Yarrow for being a model amanuensis and for her patience in typing and retyping the manuscript.

CONTENTS

INTRODUCTION

BUMMY HOLIDAY REVISITED

Today, once again, a letter has come imploring me to straighten out the record of a part of a summer—the summer of 1959—that my good friend Dom Moraes and I spent travelling together in India. Bewildered readers have been writing such letters to me ever since Dom and I published clashing accounts of our summer, each written in ignorance of the other's work. "I am a graduate student specializing in contemporary Indian literature," the latest letter to me begins. "In January and May, 1960, after you returned to the States, you wrote in the pages of *The New Yorker* about a summer in India, some of which you spent with Dom Moraes. In July and August of 1960, oddly, the *Observer* serialized an account of the same summer by Moraes after *his* return to England. Publishers in both Britain and the United States then brought out book-length accounts of the same summer by each of you.* [Here there is an actual footnote, which reads, in its entirety, "*Ved Mehta, 'Walking the Indian Streets,' Boston: Little, Brown & Co., 1960; and London: Faber & Faber, Ltd., 1961. Cf. Dom Moraes, 'Gone Away: An Indian Journey,' Boston: Little, Brown & Co., 1960; and London: William Heinemann, Ltd., 1960."] The strange thing is that even when you are describing the same experiences—the same people and the same places—your versions are poles apart, and this in spite of the fact that you were both Indians, and both going back home from Oxford. I am at a loss to understand."

I acknowledge the need for all sorts of explanations. But explaining means overcoming years of reluctance to reopen a

subject recorded and closed, and facing what I did that summer
in the light of what in later years I came to feel about it. In fact,
year after year following that summer I made plans to return to
India and then abandoned them, because I did not quite see
how I could go back without first trying to straighten out the
confusion that the 1959 visit created in my mind. But then I
resolved to revisit both the confusion and India, and I have
have done so, which has meant rereading our two reports—
Dom's "Gone Away" and my "Walking the Indian Streets."
"Gone Away" is the fatter of the two books, and, reading it, I
am once again enthralled. I feel like an old Boy revisiting his
college after many years out in the world, and, in fact the book
is full of our particular undergraduate years at Oxford—1956
through 1959. From this distance, I am naturally a little embarrassed at the cozy details of the Oxford feast that is "Gone
Away." But I am comforted by the presence at the feast of E. M.
Forster, who joins it as a reviewer of the book for the *Observer*.
Forster tells approvingly of a talk he once had with Dom. "When
I met Mr. Moraes some years ago, he made a remark that both
surprised and pleased me," he says, a bit donnishly. "He had
lent me some of his poems, and when accepting them I said
rather conventionally : 'I'll write to you about them.' To which
he replied, with perfect courtesy : 'I do not wish you to write
about them. I wish you to read them.' It was a sound remark and
it recalled me to essentials." Having noted that "Gone Away,"
though not unpoetical, is essentially a journal, and therefore a
piece of journalism, and that it deserves to be discussed as well
as read, Forster gives Dom a one-sentence character reference,
calling him "an excellent mixer, if occasionally farouche," and
adds quickly that the book is "an excellent mixture . . . irrever-
ent, gay, unexpected, besides being what the shops call 'contemporary' ('You may not like this pattern, sir, it is rather contemporary')." According to Forster, the question of the pattern's
durability doesn't arise, because Dom is just journalistically
describing a few months he spent in India following four years'
absence. Forster agreeably compliments his host on his reputation
as a poet—the result of a small volume of poems called "A

Beginning " and published when Dom was an undergraduate—
and mentions the influence on Dom of his father, Frank Moraes,
who is an Oxford graduate himself and an eminent Indian
journalist. However, Forster goes on to compete with his host,
remarking, in the best Forsterian manner, " I appreciated his
account of his visit to the Calcutta painter Jamini Roy, for it
recalls my own visit fifteen years ago. Indeed, I wish to enter
into competition at this point and to inform the *Observer* that
Jamini Roy gave me one of his pictures. It is a blue farmer or
maybe a god, holding a little bird, and a most treasured pos-
session. Mr. Moraes got only three kings in a boat." Then, at
that undergraduate banquet of ours, Forster taps me on the
shoulder: "Part of the time he is with Mr. Ved Mehta, his
talented contemporary at Oxford who is now on *The New
Yorker.* Now the pace quickens. A pair of gifted gigglers, they
hire a taxi and drive through the brothel district of Calcutta to
tease the prostitutes and pimps. This is not a great success. Perhaps they did not drink enough champagne first." I bristle; I am
a moderate drinker, and even have long stretches of teetotalism.
Forster, possibly knowing this, shifts his censorious look to Dom:
"He is always drinking, which becomes a bore. On the opening
page of the book brandy is mentioned twice, whiskey three times,
and this continues until the reader longs for a non-alcoholic
edition."

When the review appeared, I wished that I could tell Forster
exactly how it was that in Dom's book I became a giggler in
those escapades, but, as I have said, for years I was reluctant to
reopen the subject. Now that I am speaking up, I say to Forster
—as though the "Gone Away" banquet had been reconvened
for an anniversary—that, the last time around, he was a credu-
lous guest as well as an honored one. I explain, "You must
remember it was a smashing holiday—could be nothing less if I
was to keep my sanity in India. Or so it seemed at the time. I
had been living the life of an expatriate in America and England
for ten years. I had left my home in New Delhi in 1949, at the
age of fifteen, to start my education abroad. As you can imagine,
greeting the members of my family—a large one—after ten

years was not easy, although, just out of Oxford, I was loath to admit it, even to myself. At King's, even more than at my college, Balliol, you know one would jeer at anyone looking for a shoulder to cry on. So Dom found me in Delhi, longing for Oxford, ready for anything. We went on some of the escapades described in 'Gone Away,' it's true, in a spirit of frantic high holiday; other things Dom brought in because, I suppose, he carried his holiday spirit into his writing. So I appear as a mixture of Sancho Panza and Dr. Watson, marvelling at the feats of my inspired friend. But one thing at a time."

I next turn to Dom and tell him that in spite of my embarrassment now at some of the things recounted in "Gone Away," I am spellbound by the prose. Some of his similes would leave most novelists gasping. And I am, of course, especially entranced by the passages that concern us directly. I remind him that in India we met at Claridge's in New Delhi, in which his father kept a room as a pied-à-terre and lived as if he were still an undergraduate at Oxford. All the same, Dom was not in the best of spirits when he thought of telephoning me. As he told it in "Gone Away":

> When I went across to my father's room [Dom had his own room at Claridge's], it was already full of the beginnings of the train of visitors who appear, as if answering the Pied Piper's flute, wherever he goes. . . . American, English, and Indian journalists were scattered with glasses of whiskey all over the room, comparing notes : the telephone kept ringing. I decided to strike out on my own a bit. I knew that Ved Mehta was in Delhi, so I looked up his parents' number and called him. . . . I got him on the line, after some trouble explaining my identity to the servant, and an astonished voice said : " Is that really you, Dommie?" This is the name that I was always called by the more whimsical of my Oxford friends : it was originally given me by a little boy. "Yes," I said.
> "What are you doing here?"
> "I'll tell you," I said, " if you come and have a drink with me." So we arranged to meet that evening. . . . I opened my eyes next morning with pain and care, one at a time. . . . The door opened and Ved came in, looking terrifyingly spruce.
> "Ved," I said, dazedly, " where am I?"

"You're in the spare bedroom of my house, dear boy. Don't you remember? No, I don't suppose you do."

"I haven't done anything awful, have I?"

"It depends," Ved replied judicially, "what you call awful."

He added, "You were pretty sloshed when I arrived, Dommie, and you kept talking about the Defence Ministry. After that you gave a lecture on Anglo-Saxon poetry. I never knew you knew so much about it. Everybody there was fascinated, and there were hundreds of people there. Then I thought a little dinner would be good for you, so we went out. Then came the dog."

"What dog?"

"We found a stray dog on the street. You wanted to take it into the restaurant for dinner, but they wouldn't let you. But you still seemed to think it was there. In fact, you put all your dinner under the table for it. The man at the next table went rushing to the telephone to call up his friends. He wanted to tell them that they ought not to miss it, it was the only time this was likely to happen in Delhi. I told him that if you stuck around here for a few days, Dommie, the novelty would be sure to wear off."

I buried my head in my hands.

"Never mind. Have a cold shower and some breakfast. Then we have some business. There were a lot of writers who came to meet you, but you didn't give them much opportunity. Unless they've changed their minds, I think we should call on them this morning." . . . In the taxi I said, "Your parents are charming. I do hope I haven't shocked them."

"Oh no," Ved said. "There was only one thing they thought a little strange. When we arrived here last night I introduced you to my mother, and you clasped her hand and said, 'I'm delighted to meet you. I've heard so much about you, sir.'"

I take Dom to task a little—still in the spirit of the anniversary feast, "Some troglodyte points: I never called you 'Dommie' or 'dear boy.' There was no Anglo-Saxon-poetry lecture. In any case, a dozen people would have been too many for a Claridge's room. We met no stray dog, and, by the way, to my mother 'sir' and 'madam' would have been equally strange, since her small, charming vocabulary in English at the time did not include either form of address. Of course, my version of this meeting of ours, in 'Walking the Indian Streets,' is a little different—though the experience of reading my own printed account of it is even stranger than the experience of reading yours." I furnish chapter and verse :

The telephone rings and penetrates the educative process [" educative process " because before the telephone call I have been seeing family, villagers, political and religious leaders, and bystanders, and trying to come to terms with sunstroke, heat, flies and starving millions]. " This is me ! " says a voice. " Hello, it's you, on the phonekins," I reply, and Oxford is in India [" kins " because, in our talk at Oxford, Dom and I and our other friends occasionally attached " kins " to words in order to make our speech rhythmic and characteristically ours]. . . . He settles into a room in a posh hotel, and fills the cabinet with nectar—drinks for him and tiny drinks for me. [" Tiny " is like " kins," also for rhythm, etc.] . . . First thing we do after some drinking is to go to the Volga, a bourgeois Delhi place with upper-class pretensions. Dom is slightly unmanageable. I order a four-course dinner. Dom says he wants nothing to eat, but I say he must eat, because liquids without solids are bad for the health. So I order for him. Dom speaks only English, for though he was brought up in Bombay, he's had much less Indian background than I. I am at home in three Indian languages and so can order conveniently. Dom accidentally splashes soup on my suit, then feeds a tiny bit of rice to imaginary dogs under the table. I am embarrassed but enjoy being the center of attention. A Sikh at the far-left table picks up the phone, dials a number, then tries, in Punjabi, to persuade someone to come to the Volga immediately. " You can't imagine what is going on here," he says. " Just come for five minutes." (The fool doesn't realize that I can understand Punjabi.) Dom then feeds a tiny bit of pudding to the imaginary dogs. The waiters don't know what to do. The orchestra starts playing conservative English melodies as loudly and furiously as possible. We stagger out, to everyone's relief, and get a taxi and order the driver to take us to my home.

I hasten to add, in talking to Dom, " But your version may, in spirit, be much more like ' uskins' on that tiny holiday." Again I supply the reference from " Walking the Indian Streets " :

We seldom told an unvarnished truth; we made whatever happened to us more fanciful and funny, to amuse ourselves and our friends. (In this Dom was more gifted than I, but he brought out my playful self.) This was not necessarily intentional. It was just part of our natures, or perhaps, more accurately, it was an escape from our natures. Both of us wore heavy armor, and our nonsense shielded us from the public, and from each other, and from ourselves. This is, in fact, to say that the friendship between Dom and me was English—reserved, witty, sarcastic, intellectual, and sometimes uncommunicative, if you took words alone as an index of feelings.

"Of course, Dom," I continue, "in Delhi I was with my family and you were with your father, so we did not see as much of each other as we might have during our bummy days at Oxford, say." From "Walking the Indian Streets":

At Oxford, we worked frightfully hard perhaps for five or six days, five or six weeks, and after this intensive period we took a physical and spiritual holiday, bumming and being amiable, visiting and being visited. These bummy days were an Oxford specialty. Just as some people have Sabbath days, we had bummy days. They are necessary to those of us who lead serious lives day in and day out, like ants on the pages of a folio musty with age and use.

"The pace naturally quickened as we raced, in a very bummy fashion, through Nepal and Calcutta. In Katmandu, thanks to a letter of introduction from your father, we were invited to stay at the palace of a Rana"—the Ranas being members of the Nepalese aristocracy. "Your description of our arrival there is wild."

My reference is to this passage from "Gone Away":

"Coo, Dommie!" Ved said. "This really is a palace."
At this point I became aware of an enormous Himalayan bear crouched next to the sofa. It glowered at me. I gasped.
"Now what is it?"
". . . It must . . . be stuffed."
"Honestly, Dommie, I know you have a fantasy-life, but what do you think? Have you ever known anybody who kept a live bear in their drawing room?"
"I only wondered," I was beginning lamely, when the bear rose, snarled at us, and shambled loosely out through the farther door.

B

"Coo! I am moved now to coo, Dom—for the first time in my life—because, leaving aside my ingenuous comment, we were never once accosted during our stay in the palace by so much as a Teddy bear. But in your account the exit of the imaginary bear is beautifully orchestrated with the arrival of our hostess, the Rani, and, of course, you immediately tackle her on the subject of the bear. 'There was a bear here a few minutes ago,' you say to the Rani." I continue to quote from "Gone Away":

> "Ah yes," said the Rani dreamily. "Which bear?"
> "You have several?"
> "Oh yes. That is one thing you must be careful about: don't go out at night; they don't see very well in the dark, and they might not know you were guests."

"The chimerical bear has multiplied, Dom. In fact, when we talked about how grand it would have been to live in the palace of a Rana at the noon of his feudal power, I had no idea that, writing of our experiences in Nepal, you would make out that many things perhaps present a hundred years ago were still about now—as though the DC-3 that carried us to Katmandu were a time machine. But how the modern Ranas must wish that they were still living in the palace of your description!"

Making a guide of one of our host's sons, an engineer, Dom continues the report of our first day's adventures:

> He led us down to the ground floor. It was a long way.
> "Who lives in these five hundred rooms?"
> "Well, my father has five of us, you know. Five sons. We each have quarters for ourselves and our families. Then lots of the rooms are guest-rooms, drawing-rooms, that kind of thing. And of course the maidservants have one wing."
> "Maidservants?" inquired Ved. The engineer son laughed and inserted an elbow into Ved's ribs. "We had more of them before 1951, of course. About two hundred and fifty. Now I think the actual number is about a hundred and fifty. Useful girls, they do everything, ha ha!" The elbow drove into my ribs this time.
> We went out through a carved wooden porch into the main courtyard. The palace was rectangular and the courtyard a rectangle within a rectangle. It was very busy: men and women in

loose tunics and felt shoes moveu ceaselessly through it—the servants : the women almost all young and pretty. And on three sides
of the courtyard there were shops. There were a blacksmith and
a goldsmith, a cobbler, a tailor, a barber, a dispensary, and, in
one corner, an anonymous doorway to which the engineer son
pointed.

"That's the most important of all. The bank."

He nudged Ved again, laughing.

"Who uses these shops?"

He looked at me, surprised. "Why, we do. The family. We pay
all these people and they serve us."

"What's the idea?" Ved said.

"When these palaces were built the Ranas had the idea of setting up autonomous communities in each one. All these people
live in our house, and we take care of them. We feed and clothe
them, and they serve us. It is like a little city. We even have a
school in the grounds, for their children."

The "Gone Away" hospitality, thanks to that time machine,
is every bit up to the "Gone Away" palace. According to Dom,
our host, the General (all the top Ranas have the title of general),
bidding us good night on our first evening, said, "I hope I have
not forgotten anything that would make you comfortable."

"Oh no, sir," we said. . . .

When, at about midnight, we stumbled back to our room, we
found Pannalal [one of the palace servants] asleep across the doorway. We stepped over him. "Do you want the light, Dommie?"

"No," I said.

We undressed in the dark. Ved was quicker than I was. He
moved over to his bed while I was still fastening my pyjama
trousers. I heard him struggling through the mosquito-curtain,
and then came a yell of horror.

My first thought was of stray bears. I rushed to the light-switch
and turned it on. Ved was scrambling out of his bed, which now
contained a very pretty Nepalese girl. She didn't have any clothes
on. When I turned to my bed, there was one there too. She laughed
and made an unmistakable gesture.

Pannalal had now woken up. He stood doomfully in the door,
wiping the sleep out of his eyes.

"What are these girls doing here?" I said.

"The General Sahib sent them to entertain you. If they are not pretty enough, I will fetch two others."

"No, no," I said, and cravenly retired into the dining-room, leaving Ved to cope with the situation.

When I returned, the girls had gone. Pannalal, looking very indignant, was going back to sleep.

"How did you get rid of them?" I asked admiringly.

"I said we both had a contagious disease."

"Genius," I said.

"Just a knack, just a knack, nothing at all," Ved said, crawling back through the mosquito-curtain. "Poof, they use very strong scent."

I now reproach Dom with: "The events of this day—as of many others described in the book—are all poof. If such a day had been conjured up for your friends at Oxford, we would have been impressed by your powers of make-believe but at some point or other we would have said, 'Good tale,' and, the enchantment broken, gone on to have a drink. Treating every poor reader as an Oxford friend lays you open, I'm afraid, to a charge of misplaced generosity. Actually, you are even more bountiful to me. Still leafing through the Nepalese section, I find myself performing an equestrian feat that I could scarcely have managed strapped to the back of a winged mule." Once more, I quote from "Gone Away":

Three sidling ponies stood, saddled, but rolling crimson nostrils, and gently and angrily flattening their ears.

In the midst of their pirouettes, we seized them, I feeling piratical, and came aboard. The saddles were wooden and horned, and hurt as soon as one sat on them. . . . It was midday. . . . I felt slightly anxious about Ved. As I bounced on the wooden saddle, I decided I must keep an eye on him. I was much aggrieved when he came cantering back down the bridle-path.

"Are you okay, Dommie? Do you want a hand?"

"No," I said sourly, and followed the other two thereafter. [The third rider he has introduced simply as "Gupta."]

The road was steep, rock-strewn, and occasionally flooded. Progress was slow. Every now and then the ponies had to tip toe along the edge of a precipice. At first it was all right: the precipice was low to the ground, and a fall would have meant a cut elbow, perhaps, and reminded one happily of one's childhood. Later it grew higher; a fall would have meant a broken neck. My pony insisted on the edge, and I kicked it despairingly. Occasionally, squinting down, I would see clods disintegrate from its hoof and its previous foothold rain down crumbwise into the valley beneath.

All round the mountains got bigger, hairier, more menacing, and the valley dwindled to small Chinese roofs and rivers like saliva-threads from the sudden lips of the hills. I held the reins, pressed my knees tight into the pony's sparse ribs, and hoped. Finally we emerged from the edge into an area of trotted-up slopes, the trees steaming mist on either side. I had to lean forward on the pony to keep in sight of the others, and also, with the mist steaming in through my shirt, it became exceedingly cold.

"Are you all right?" Gupta shouted back through the mist, and I replied haughtily, "Excellent."

Then more climbing. The pony stuttered his feet every so often, and yawed his head back, and squiggled his behind, and riding became agony. The mist had fortunately blotted out any prospects of a fall, and my entire consciousness was concentrated on avoiding the next bump. Eventually we climbed to a village, where people came out and stared amazedly. . . .

"Come on, Dommie," said Ved enthusiastically, still from the saddle. "We must go."

We did, then, scrambling up a steep track dissolving now in the faint mountain rain, always higher; the wooden saddle unbearable each time the pony trotted : but luckily that wasn't often.

Finally, in the mist, the ponies clinging with slithery hooves to the edge, lights glimmered in the stew ahead. . . . So I stuck my heels into the pony's side again, and managed to arrive, at a species of canter, in a village of nervous mud huts sticking to the mountain. People came out to stare. We dismounted and looked around.

"Now then," I protest to Dom. "For the three or four days we were in Nepal, we stayed put most of the time in our tiny palace in Katmandu, and didn't go near a horse, though the names of several villages we supposedly rode through—Patan, Bhatgaon, Thoka—did come up in our conversations with Nepalese. In fact, most of the scenes in your account of our Nepal excursions I can recognize as having been drawn from one chance remark or another, or else from stories told to us, since our ability to amuse others made them want to amuse us. Wishes have indeed become horses, but in this instance it is the reader who, not having had the privilege of meeting you, is taken for the heroic ride. What makes 'Gone Away' live for me is an occasional scene that is as dull as used college silver and china after dinner but as filling as that food that was. I admire such a tableau as your interview with the Dalai Lama, who, all the same, comes across as an aspirant to Oxford with almost the fervor of Jude the Obscure."

I was surprised [Dom reports] to find him actually a sturdy, broad-shouldered, tall young man. . . . His brown robe was open at the neck to reveal a tan shirt. He came forward and gave me an extremely firm handshake. . . . He gestured and said in English, "Please sit."

It was an enormous sofa. I sank into it with trepidation. The Dalai Lama sat beside me and the interpreter drew up a chair facing us. The Dalai Lama crossed his legs composedly, revealing under the robe brown brogues and a pair of red socks with yellow stripes. . . . "Is there any secular literature in Tibet? The recent revolt, for instance, did that produce any literature?"

The interpreter translated this. He addressed the Dalai Lama as "Kundun," his usual Tibetan title, which means "Presence." . . . Kundun thought carefully, and then answered.

"His Holiness says that he does not know of any literature, but there may be some." . . . He leant forward, tapped me on the knee, and said something. "His Holiness thanks you for your interest in the Tibetan people. He hopes to be able to send some of the young men of his people to your university, to Oxford, and to other Western universities. He will see if he is able to afford, and if possible he will send." . . .

"Can His Holiness remember his childhood before he was chosen as Lama? . . . Did he feel any different to other children?"

The Dalai Lama looked thoughtful at this. The long hands moved as though sketching a childhood in the air. But he shook his head.

"His Holiness has no particular memory of that part of his life. He cannot tell if he felt any different from other children, because he had no standards of comparison. But his mother always said that he was the noisiest child she had ever seen. . . . He asks you what you studied at Oxford."

I said Literature. The Dalai Lama nodded. The next question was about the methods of instruction. I explained the tutorial system. Again he nodded.

"Kundun thinks this is a good method. He asks you to describe the life in Oxford."

So I found myself explaining scouts, landladies, the importance of the pub, the bicycle, and the river. The Dalai Lama listened to all this closely. . . .

"Does he plan to travel a lot?"

The Dalai Lama for the first time looked sad. His hands lay inert in his lap as he spoke. "Kundun says that he cannot be interested in travel except in so far as it will help his country. He may visit some of the Buddhist countries, and if the Tibetan case is brought before the U.N., he may go to America, but he will always make India his base, and always return to it, because it is near his country. . . .

We all stood up and the Dalai Lama dropped his arm round my shoulders in a friendly gesture. . . . He shook my hand with the same firm clasp as before, and stepped aside. I remembered what I had been told about not turning my back. I accordingly began to sidle out backward, crab-fashion. The Dalai Lama watched me for a moment. Then he suddenly took a few steps forward, dropped his hands to my shoulders, and turned me round so that I faced the door.

But it's time to end the feast, and speed the guests, for I can hear Dom say to those assembled—probably with a philosophical shrug—"He that is without sin among you, let him first cast a stone." In any case, none of us can ever hope to tie up all the loose ends in "Gone Away." Kingsley Martin, writing something of a spoilsport review of the book in the *New Statesman*, caught at one of the ends when he noted, "He [Dom] muddles fact and fiction. To confuse ostensibly factual reporting by making his friends and hosts participate in fictitious and sometimes discreditable incidents is unjustifiable as art, fun, or journalism." Yet Martin could only conclude, "You have to sort out the mélange for yourself." An Indian reviewer set about doing precisely this.

He went to the length of dispatching questionnaires to many of the characters who figured in the pages of " Gone Away." One of the recipients was Jawaharlal Nehru, who was asked whether, to prolong his interview with Moraes, he had actually said, as Moraes reported in " Gone Away," " Parliament can wait for a few minutes." "The reply," the reviewer reported, "charming, evasive, characteristically Nehruvian, says that he 'has not seen Dom Moraes' book "Gone Away."' In fact, he has no recollection of any 'casual remarks' that might have been made to Mr. Moraes. 'It is possible' that he might have said, 'Parliament can wait for a few minutes,' but he is 'not quite sure.' In case he did make that remark, 'it did not mean that Parliament would be kept waiting, but that he would go there 'a few minutes later.'" The reviewer could only remark, by way of a moral, "Much virtue in 'if,' said Touchstone! And also, we might note, in 'in case.'" The other replies to the questionnaire, which the reviewer printed solemnly, along with Nehru's, in a periodical appropriately called *Quest*, were no more illuminating, and, defeated by the mélange, he could only lean on the Bible and mumble in parenthetical despair, "'What is truth?' said Pilate."

To me, as critic pro tempore, it was clear—even before I read the literary and epistolary comment on " Gone Away"—from its point of view, from its imagery, and from its rhapsodic tone, that the central fact about the book was that Dom was a lyric poet whose governing intention was to indulge in undisguised hyperbole. As a friend in aeternum, I recall the Indian setting of our journey as merely a foil for our splendid bummy holiday, and I reflect that if Dom and I had been able to spend more time in India together—possibly giving him a chance to talk his book out with me in a few conversational jags (our version of the dialectic)—the bummy holiday might have yielded, when it reached print, a cluster of pure memories instead of the mélange. As things have actually worked out, our Indian journey of 1959, and the confusion growing out of it, might just as well have been swept aside, for it is as though we had never been there that summer, and the actual India (the India that has one-sixth of the world's population and one-half of the world's democratic population) were still waiting to be discovered. But looking to the future, I wish to remember, above all, an exchange I had with Dom—reported in "Gone Away"—as we were saying goodbye in Calcutta in the rain; I was leaving India to do postgraduate work in the United States, and he was to do some further travelling in India and then go back to England to write poetry. He said that one day we would each return to India, but "older, stiffer, and more settled." (Later on, I read in manuscript Dom's subsequent prose work, an autobiography called "My Son's Father." As in "Gone Away," so in "My Son's Father," Dom writes about his doings in India and England—his travels, his adventures, his romances, his entanglements with high society and low life—giving, throughout, his impressions of poets, writers, journalists, painters, actors, Oxford contemporaries. As in the first book, so in the second book, I know many of the people he writes about, was present at many of the scenes he describes, and recall many of the conversations he records. But in "My Son's Father," perhaps because of the seven years of self-discovery that separate the writing of the two books, the reporting seems to me quite straight. Indeed, the frankness of the new book reminds me of the autobiography of Stephen Spender.) I think now that he might have said, "Sadder, too," for our antics, the elements of friendship that supported them, the ability to create from the hush of our fancies a cozy island in the sea of misery around us—these have now all been put away.

I

HOMECOMING

A letter from an ancient and religious aunt who has ignored my existence for many years arrives in the morning post. "Dear Child," it reads. "You will be coming home to India after ten years. How you must have grown. I hope you are still my fifteen-year-old darling and love me as you did before. I think about how Ram came home, after fourteen years' banishment, having fought and conquered evil in the jungles, and the people enjoyed and celebrated his return with candles and with bonfires. They say that when he returned the earth glowed like the sun. I hope you still remember and read the 'Ramayana,' our great religious epic. Maybe you don't, though. Boys get corrupted by the West. . . ." My old aunt goes on, but I really haven't time to read the letter properly. I am just in the middle of studying for my Oxford finals, reading the notes on four-by-six index cards. I put the letter beside me and start on the cards. I go through hundreds of them, dealing with Alfred, with John and Henry VIII, with Elizabeth, Cromwell, and Gladstone. There isn't any time for my aunt, so I bury her among my index cards, along with other late Hanoverians.

I ought to explain that if I had received the same letter two years ago it would have been an occasion for self-analysis and self-mortification. It would have made me look at myself in my mental mirror, and I would not have enjoyed watching the image there. I would have brooded over my shortcomings. But in these two years something has happened to me. The previous intensity of my feelings seems to have faded into the leisurely habits of Oxford. When I arrived at Oxford, after living in America for seven years, I was crew-cut innocence abroad. I sprang out of bed at the healthy hour of seven, drank milk with breakfast, lunch, and dinner, and was in bed before midnight. I submitted to the influences of Oxford when I started breaking up my afternoon work with a cup of tea at four. Then followed a cup of coffee after dinner. Sometimes I let myself be persuaded to coffee after lunch also. Then came sherry before dinner, first on weekends, then on weekdays. I enjoyed, now and again, taking some wine with dinner and brandy with coffee, and on special occasions, like a good party, I was prevailed upon to take punch with a gin base, or even a Scotch. I never drank very much, because it made me feel tired, and also because the pressure of work never let up. When I did take a coffee or tea break, or have a beer in Hall, I often became less serious and intense, more social and convivial. And this was splendid, because friendships and attachments came easily, and I abandoned introspection for gossip and wit. The English apparently know how to be casual and witty at the same time. For my part, I sometimes found the strain of making witty remarks too much, but by persevering I developed the ability to pick up a remark and turn it in a funny and unexpected direction. Often the wit was the result of clever, clever me, and when I was being unusually clever, I controlled the wit as if I were working marionettes. Sometimes, stringing along with the wooden English figures, I performed feats I little expected, and while I never thought all this was really changing me in any radical way, in time I became adept at exploiting my fancies. I began feeling that, somehow, there were two me's. The playful me did not make the serious me less dependable (just less vulnerable), and I came to see a quick, satirical wisdom in my own foolishness.

So, you see, my aunt's letter in the middle of finals is extremely inconvenient. But when they are over, I start to look for it. In memory, it seems to be more Indian than anything I have received from home in some years, and although I haven't read the "Ramayana" recently, I begin to think I should.

But, before that, summer clothes. I go down to my tailors,

distinguished tailors for young English gentlemen, and ask them
to fit me out with some summer clothes. "Now, sir," the cutter
says to me. "I understand you are going to the tropics. How
would you like a Prince of Wales design? That is what we sold
to the last aide-de-camp of the Viceroy, and there has never been
any complaint." However, I want something simple. "Then,
sir," the cutter replies, "I recommend some fawn-colored
material. It is quite appropriate." I remind the cutter that I am
really an Indian, and, when in India, want, as far as possible, to
be taken for an Indian, and not a dandified actor. We settle on
an honest tropical wool. The cutter and the tailor attend me
in a side room. The tailor surveys me squint-eyed. I feel like an
object about to be cunningly displayed. Some time later, when I
pick up the suit, I find I am a bit embarrassed wearing it. The
honest wool has been subtly altered.

The evening before my flight to India, a Pakistani gentleman
who is a stranger to me comes to bid me goodbye. My artistic
suit hangs in the clothes-press; he wears his. I am interested in
him as a guide to what I can expect at home, for recently he,
too, has returned. Like an American who sits next to you in a
train, he easily unfolds his story. After his years at an English
university, an English firm offered him a job. He refused it for
nationalistic reasons and joined the Pakistani Civil Service, at
one-third the English salary. Some of his Anglophobe superiors
hated him for being a gentleman and posted him in a forsaken
district of an unfamiliar province. Part of his duty consisted of
dispensing justice, and he felt he was good at this, because of his
English education. The Pakistanis despised him for this education
but, paradoxically, returned him to England, some years ago, for
further training; like him, they were caught between East and
West, and were torn in their loyalties.

He washes down tumblers of whiskey while I'm nursing one
social drink. He went home to serve his country and returned to
England an alcoholic. "I've always loved my women and my
whiskey, but in my district there are no women," he explains. "I
dispensed licenses for the whiskey, so I gave myself five bottles
of Scotch a month, which cost twice my Civil Service pay. But

my daddy paid with his black-market money, which I self-indulgently accepted." In preparing himself for service in Pakistan, he tried to give up drink. But he found no support or encouragement in Pakistan; the time hung heavy and the evenings were numb with inactivity. "I still tried to give it up," he insists, "but at six o'clock a thousand bells would ring in my head, something would happen to the pupils of my eyes, I would feel tired, and my head would ache." Drinking for Muslims is like eating beef for Hindus, so he couldn't drink in public. "At six," he confesses, "I would lock the doors, pull down the shades, and pour out a quarter of a bottle into a big mug. I would turn on the 'Voice of America' and start drinking my way out of Pakistan. When I began to feel merry, I would dance a lonely dance to the 'Voice of America' music. I despised myself, but I couldn't help it. I would eat late—at eleven, twelve o'clock. I would nurse the mug as long as I could. You can't keep whiskey secret from your bearer. 'Sahib,' my bearer said to me one day, 'we expected people to be drunkards during the British raj, but we thought that in our new Islamic republic things would be different.' I had to frighten him; he held my job and my reputation in his hands at that moment. The government won't keep you if they know you drink. I went over to the sideboard and picked up two empty whiskey bottles. 'If you say another word about this,' I screamed, 'I will crack your head open with these bottles!' Sobbing, the bearer fell at my feet, kissed my boots, and prayed to Mohammed. I have never done anything so horrible in my life. All my education—what was it for?"

Pain throbs in my friend's whiskey-soaked eyes. I feel the terrible alienation imposed on him by his English clothes and his English vision. Drink befogs the issue but cannot dull the pain. He leaves me depressed and reflective.

Everyone must belong, yet those of us who were born in the twilight of the British raj were wounded for life. As children, we were intimidated by well-spoken English and we were flattered by invitations to play at English houses, because we were told that these invitations were a mark of the highest success. We grew up thinking that white men were better than brown men, that a dark child in the family was less blessed than one with a fairer complexion. We grew up with a dream of going to England and catching a glimpse of the Oxford and Cambridge spires. The setting of the British sun left us with an intellectual contempt for English values, but emotionally we were too far committed to withdraw, and our whole generation was sacrificed to a country in transition. We were condemned to live with a permanent hangover. My Pakistani friend is not alone in having no sense of belonging.

I barely catch the plane. We go up and up. The atmosphere is stifling, and the presence of the Anglo-Indian hostesses annoying. England drops away beneath the wings, and India, the India I knew years ago, explodes in my consciousness. Painful memories stand out: Uncertain freedom in 1947, and misgivings about whether the country will be politically and economically viable. Partition in 1947, and Hindus and Sikhs murdered or dispatched by the million to India; partition in 1947, and Muslims murdered or fleeing homeless by the million to Pakistan; partition in 1947, and more millions of Muslims choosing to remain in Gandhi's India. January 30, 1948, India deprived of a great leader and a saint. Prime Minister Nehru, bent from the blow, pronounced, "The light has gone out of our lives." Then there are years of estrangement: waiting in foreign places and asking questions about Gandhi's secular and casteless India, asking questions about changes—in the Constitution, in leadership, in economics. There are also personal memories, textbook history involved with family recollections: we, Hindus living in Pakistan, were forced to flee, leaving behind us all our property and our faith in the ability of Hindu and Muslim ever to live side by side.

I must now get everything into focus. It is not easy to find a way back home after a long absence. There are the subtle national changes. There is the aging and breaking up of the family—the death of my grandmother, the marriages of many. There is the alienation of education and vocabulary, of time and space.

Prague is called, then Rome, Beirut. In Damascus, I get off the plane and order coffee. Flies as fat as rats catch sight of me

with their four thousand eyes. They sit on my nose, brush my
eyelashes, caress my forehead. "Never mind the coffee," I say,
and I rush back to the plane.

Vast stretches of the Indian Ocean move into view. It is hard
to see from the plane. What can be seen, but barely, are the
hundreds of ships, their flags flying high, carrying silks, spices,
and jewels to imperial England.

Cinema India, the India I have lived with in the years of exile,
slides into focus. The voice is the narrator's, the English is the
Queen's, and the accent is unmistakably upper-class:

"India is a land of paradoxes, contradictions, extremes. On the
one hand, there are the Himalayan ranges—fifteen hundred miles
across, thousands of feet high, almost as cold as the Antarctic.
On the other, there is the Deccan, as flat as the desert, three
months hot and nine months hotter still. There is the Gangetic
plain, as fertile as any delta. There are heat waves and monsoons.
The parching sun and four hundred inches of rain a year. The
poverty of the people and the rich extravagances of the mahara-
jahs (six hundred wasteful and dissipated principalities before
India's independence). Clubs as leisurely as any in St. James's,
and slums as squalid as any in the East End. The Gandhi, ascetic
India and the begging, hungry India. The brown northerners,
of Aryan stock, with straight hair, blue or brown eyes, thin lips,
clear features—all the marks of successful invaders. And the
Negroid southerners—fugitive Dravidians from the Gangetic
plain, with kinky hair, turned-up noses, and thick lips. This is
India.

"Here are its religions. Mohammedans, physical and militant,
turn their eyes five times a day westward to Mecca. Fraternal,
like their Semitic brethren, they give unquestioning and complete
obedience to the mullah and the mosque. They believe in God
and have one sacred book; their Heaven is rich with physical
adornments—oases flowing with milk and honey—and Omar
Khayyám is their sensuous philosopher. They believe that all
non-believers, whether shown the light or not, are heretics and
damned. These are the Mohammedans. This is India. Here are
the Hindus: More gods than can sit on Olympus. No single book.

An eclectic belief in universal salvation, the same for murderers and saints, monkeys and bears. Indisputable reverence for life in any form—life purified through cycles of reincarnation. And, with this reverence for life, this belief in salvation for all, the caste system. These are the Hindus. This is India.

"This is the caste system, whose origins lie in history and religion. The conquering Aryans made slaves of the Dravidians in the Gangetic plain. The Dravidians fled south and enslaved the aborigines. Brown Aryans, black Dravidians, blacker aborigines—this is the source of caste and class. This invidious system becomes part and parcel of the Hindu cycle of reincarnation. A social issue becomes a burning religious question. This is the caste system. This is India.

"India's history encompasses saint and savage : Buddha, the high priest of non-violence, and Asoka, the greatest and godliest of the world's emperors, and then Mahmud of Ghazni, hit-and-run conqueror and Mohammedan auctioneer of Hindu women. Passive, peaceful India stands still in front of his assault, yields gradually to his Mohammedan successors. Most Indian Mohammedans are converts from Hinduism; converted rule the unconverted in the magnificent Moghul empire. Then decline of empire, India racked with disunity, the East India Company, the Sepoy Mutiny of 1857, the sun of the British Empire. In the twentieth century, renaissance at last, led by Tagore and Gandhi. World wars fan the fire of liberation. This is India.

"New and old jostle each other. Astrology and astronomy. Ancient ruins and modern wonders. Newly uncovered archaeological treasures and new air-conditioned trains. This is India."

Great stuff. This is cinema India. This is skin-deep and depthless India.

New Delhi is announced, and the plane bends down, dives, glides, and then comes to a dead halt. More than a hundred relatives have gathered for the ceremony of my return. From a distance, they seem indistinct, and I have lost their faces in the years of separation. As I leave the plane and walk toward them, they pelt me with flowers. I stand there circled with garlands, which,

C

like snowdrifts, rise from my feet to my eyebrows. I am impris-
oned in the circle of flowers and relatives. Then I am swept away,
and dozens of beggars following our progress through the flowers
are rewarded with coins. The beggars, invoking the gods to bless
our munificence, disperse with cheerful faces. We are all bundled
into old cars and, like a marriage procession, amble across the
hot plains toward the city and home.

At home, things are different. All the houses in the colony are
newly built, and their modest façades remind me that I am one
of the refugees from Pakistan. Our new home is a feeble shadow
of the old—small, without a compound, and with two, rather
than a dozen, servants.

The rites of welcome continue at home. Sweetmeats, previously
blessed, are served to all, and music is needed. The music master
sits in the center of the drawing room, beside his harmonium. I
recall him from Pakistani days, and greet him by touching his
feet. He sweeps all the relatives aside, looks at me, and preens
himself on his handiwork. "I taught him music when he was
five. I was his first master!" he exclaims. He makes me sit down
on the floor beside him, and then rapidly and nervously performs
his songs. Distant relatives, one by one, straggle away, pressing
remembrances and invitations upon me. Young nieces and
nephews are put to bed. While three brothers-in-law and a new
sister-in-law stand in waiting, the original family, the refugees
from Pakistan, weave around the music master a garland of
praise.

Now the master breaks into songs reminiscent of happier days.
Warming his voice at the past, he sings long-forgotten melodies.
There are battle marches and coy wedding songs; women at the
well sing in the springtime; a child lost from his mother calls;
farmers snip the corn with crisp tunes; a mother mourns at the
funeral of her child and prays to God for his good reincarnation.
We are carried back to the old family ways. My sisters, now
mothers, laugh and cry like schoolgirls. We all remember the
happy days before division and freedom.

The night draws the curtain between the past and the present,
and my sisters depart for their homes, leaving us reduced in

numbers and happiness. The music master muses, "Change is the way of the world. It stands still only in music. Schoolgirls grow up to be women, exchange books for children. All must take separate ways if they are not to grow into unhappiness together. And that is natural."

The music master, the conjurer-up of the past, leaves with his disciple, who carries the harmonium on his head. He promises to return when he can. I go to bed on the veranda, for it is too hot to sleep inside. He will return, I know, and so will my sisters, with their husbands and their children, but his music is too frail to support the old happiness always.

SITTING ON THE ISSUES

India has an uncanny way of bringing out extremes in her people. I suppose it is because we Indians have been afflicted and enriched by centuries of migrations, have been moved like pawns between this ruler and that. Our capacity for a single allegiance has been dulled. Instead, we have developed an ability to be compassionate and cruel, sensitive and callous, deep and fickle. To untrained eyes we appear colorful and picturesque; to critical eyes we appear shoddy imitations of our various masters. They miss our depth and complexity. We may have divided sensibilities, but we also have a relation between heart and head that is foreign to more civilized countries across the Indian Ocean.

The writer Han Suyin remarks somewhere that Asians are like onions. They fatten, layer upon layer, over the centuries. Strip them, layer by layer, and there are still more layers to go. I agree with her; travelling through India, I feel like an onion. There is the English me, hankering after Oxford happiness. And there is the Indian me, wishing to find a place in his own society. At first, I'm frightened of exploring too deeply. Other England-returned Indians display me eagerly as an Oxford article, and for a while it is easy to drift and drink in their society. I easily accept their judgment that there is an unconscious resentment against returned natives who have been educated abroad, and that a host of prejudices will prevent Anglicized Indians from becoming natives. It is easier to believe than to probe with uncertain touch. But the Indian patriot nags at the English expatriate. I try to find my way back to the heart of India by walking and talking and listening to friends, politicians, and men in the crowd. I have never felt the press of problems and people as I feel it here. I can't walk the streets. They are crowded with venders, hawkers, servants shopping for their masters, little boys getting their education from gaunt men who seem to know everything about life and who laugh cunningly as they pass on the wisdom of the streets. The wisdom of my expatriate friends is more lucidly phrased. The country is diseased and overpeopled, and they blame history and the politicians. They say, "At the beginning of the century, we had a little over half the present population, just enough for the irrigated land. We had good masters in the English. They did not understand us, but they believed in justice, law, and order, and the Indians did not know English well enough to approach them with graft. The English in India weren't burdened with poor relations; most of them came to rule singly. But look around you now. Everywhere there is corruption and nepotism. Gandhi is dead, and with him our enthusiasm for freedom." Some expatriates, trying to outdo the patriots, add, "Only Communism can restore our moral confidence." They are not alone in their complaint. Each morning, the English-language papers proclaim to their educated readers, in banner headlines, news of political storms everywhere. There is Kerala and Communism, General Thimayya vs. Krishna Menon, China and yellow imperialism. The text develops the themes "Evils of Party Government," "Incurable Wrongs," and "Democracy on the Way Out."

An All India Radio broadcast claims that caste relationships remain unchanged and that Gandhi's great struggle on behalf of the untouchables, whom he called "Harijans" ("children of God"), has been lost and forgotten; the children of God are still not permitted to enter the Brahman temples. Pundits and Cassandras forecast a civil war between northern and southern India, between the so-called Aryan and Dravidian races. Fanatics in the Punjab, like Tara Singh, herald a secession movement for the Sikhs, and other fanatics in India urge a holocaust of Muslims to make the motherland safe for the Hindu majority. Someone compares Nehru in India to Noah in his ark—Noah, who by his partitions kept the lions from the lambs. Someone else says, "The outcome is uncertain." Yet another confidently predicts, "All lights will truly go out with Nehru's death." In an old Punjabi newssheet that I find covering a cupboard shelf, there is an even more fatuous prediction that, beginning in 1957, the hundredth anniversary of the Indian Mutiny, there will be twelve years of total darkness in India, during which all the Muslims will be massacred and their remains used to fertilize bumper crops. For myself, I disregard the prophecies but am disturbed by the presence of the prophets.

In my first days in Delhi, I meet a number of my family's friends, some of whom are Muslims. I am glad to see that our family, though victims of Muslim persecution, have made Muslim friends. These Muslims think of India as home, because they have known no other; they are Indians before they are Muslims. But they are concerned lest Gandhi's secular India pass, after Nehru, into the hands of fanatics and religious purists. Pakistan they regard as an unfortunate legacy of the British raj, which ultimately parcelled out the country on the theory that Hindus and Muslims would need separate nations. The theory was naïve, because Muslims were dispersed throughout India and almost half of them did not wish to be uprooted in order to create a separate nation. Kashmir, predominantly Muslim, first joined India and now would join Pakistan. The tidy British formula produced snarled loyalties and an issue to intensify the hatred between the two nations. War between Pakistan and India over Kashmir would destroy the Indian Muslims, who would not know whether to put national loyalties above religious loyalties. Even the threat of war, by keeping the Hindu-Muslim question open, jeopardizes the secular Indian state.

I catch one of these family friends and listen to his real fears, which are not discussed in the national newspapers. He works for an English firm with offices in India and Pakistan. Part of his family has emigrated to Pakistan, but so far he remains in India. His speech is fluent, his analysis keen. "Free India has treated us better than we had any right to expect, but perhaps the government has been too conciliatory and too judicious," he says. "While archaic Hindu laws on marriage and caste, for example, have been brought up to date, Muslim laws have been left untouched. Like the British, our government has been too sensitive about religious practices. I am certain that if the Hindus do not force the Muslims to reform, they will never reform themselves, and before the Muslims know it, they will be a backward minority. Then, just as the Hindus blame their social backwardness and archaic laws on the British, so the Muslims will blame theirs on the Hindus. The fault may be Muslim, but I doubt whether the cursed generations of the future will remember this. I am afraid of a Hindu raj." My Muslim friend explains to me that the newspapers can't discuss these questions openly. The eight million refugees who have fled from Pakistan since partition carry with them inflammable memories.

I find the newspapers and magazines too grim, and search them for theatre criticism and for reviews of musical events, poetry, and fiction, but there is little of that, because, as I keep reminding myself, culture needs affluence and leisure, and India is a poor country. Gossip is as abundant as light, and travels at the speed of light: "An important politician attends all his official meetings in his pajamas. He needs frequent injections, because of some internal trouble, and it is a common sight for the Civil Service grandees to see him undo his pajama cord and receive a hip injection while he is haranguing them about lapses in duty among the civil servants or about the disloyalty of corrupt sanitary inspectors." "He calls all the grandees, contemptuously, 'clerks.'" "Some of his relatives are known hooligans. They gamble, they abduct women, they live in several sins." And so the political gossip goes, until some state capitals seem political circuses and hotbeds of corruption.

I have been doing some writing for the *Statesman*, the last of the English-owned papers in India. My press card is a passport to politicians who would be inaccessible otherwise. I go to the newspaper office to turn in my copy. For my own edification, I sit and drink coffee and talk with Alfred Evan Charlton, the publisher of the Delhi edition of the *Statesman*. As an expatriate,

I find it easier to begin my political education with an Englishman who has worked on newspapers in both British and Free India. To peons, he speaks a bizarre Hindi, which I associate with the English in India. He is devoted to Nehru's India and the Commonwealth. He expatiates on India's progress. Airplanes are a great thing in India. Our country is linked and united as never before. A letter can be sent to Calcutta today and get there tomorrow, and a parliamentary committee can fly across to Madras in a few hours. The big dams will make this country more fertile than ever before, and the people will be fed. The grass-roots work of building the nation is being done everywhere—in the villages, in various kinds of schools for boys and girls, in women's colleges. Charlton has the feeling that India is producing better women than men. The reason may be that men came in more direct contact with the British raj than the women did. While the men may have been Anglicized and crippled, the women remained Indian; their seduction by the British stopped with lipstick and fingernail polish. One great strength of Gandhi's non-violent movement was the equality of men and women within it. In the West, women were liberated by industrial society, in India by passive disobedience.

I continue my political education with a visit to Rajendra Prasad, the President of India—a shy, simple leader, born and educated in India and instinctively Gandhian in his ways. I sit beside Rajendra Prasad in the stately palace built for the British Viceroys, and the saintly President seems out of place in its imperial splendor. I ask him how he entered political life and what divides British from Free India.

He reminisces. He was a successful lawyer in Bihar when Mahatma Gandhi arrived in the province to settle a labor dispute on the rice plantations. Gandhi was on the side of the workers, Prasad was on the side of the owners, and then, one day, they came together from their two different sides, and Gandhi talked to him for ten or fifteen minutes, and he was a different man. "Before I met Gandhiji, my aims, like those of all parents, were a good standard of living and the best of education for my children, and I was in a position to achieve them, but after I met him, these things that had been important earlier were important no more. My wife and children were no longer the first things in my life."

Had this meeting made him indifferent to personal happiness?

"You don't understand. After that meeting, I gave up everything to follow the movement, which gave me more personal happiness than anything before. Once I had taken up the cause, there was no time left to think about my children and their education." His giving himself to politics was a "testament to Gandhiji's miraculous power," he says, and he adds, "Gandhiji had a way of making leaders out of clay. Everyone who came in contact with him became a leader. But now he is gone."

Outside the palace of the past Viceroys, I stop and chat with the President's aide-de-camp. Prasad, he says, is the Lincoln of India; above all, he wishes to preserve the Union. Since our leaders realize that our country is torn by its Hindu, Moghul, and British images, the President always makes a point of spending Independence Day in the south, while the Prime Minister celebrates it at the Red Fort, in the north. The Red Fort is the ancient seat of the Moghuls, and, with the Taj Mahal, it stands as a monument to the glories of the Muslim empire. Today, its image must be accommodated in the new India. So it is that on Independence Day the Prime Minister climbs the ramparts of the Red Fort and, from this place of authority, talks to the people about the Union. The leaders of Free India live in the borrowed houses of Muslim and English rulers, and unless they learn to live in them comfortably, India will disintegrate.

Next, I find myself sitting across from a different kind of leader, one not schooled directly under Gandhi. He has his bare feet on the desk, a loin cloth around his waist, and a cup of tea in his hand. His thin, hairy legs seem inappropriate in the air-conditioned Whitehall atmosphere. The leader remarks that it is hard for poor Indians to fill the large offices of the British. Nevertheless, we cannot wish away British India.

But I came to hear his views on the Hindu-Muslim dispute. Nothing is more important to me than a secular India. I am afraid that the religious harmony of Nehru's India may be destroyed by Kashmir. I ask whether there was ever a time when India could have exchanged Kashmir for a piece of Pakistani territory. By settling the dispute over Kashmir, we would have made safe forever the lives of forty million Muslims now living in India, and perhaps done something to heal the breach between Hindus and Muslims, which robbed us of a united India, and even of Gandhi himself.

"No, no, we could never have compromised on Kashmir," he snaps. "Where do you start drawing the line? By feeding Pakistani appetites, you whet them, and before you know it they will demand the Red Fort. This is not the way to run a country. We are in the middle of a power struggle with Pakistan. We must be firm."

But doesn't our Kashmir policy contain the threat of war? Many people privately admit that if a plebiscite were held, Kashmir would go to Pakistan. We have already paid much more for Kashmir than it is worth to us. It doesn't seem sensible to me to apportion a large part of our small national budget for the defense of Kashmir.

He replies, "If Kashmir were divided or surrendered to Pakistan today, it would mean refugees and riots once again, and the lives of those forty million Muslims living in India would be anything but safe."

I insist that the Kashmir issue, unresolved, will always hold this threat and that in preferring a status quo to a permanent settlement we are merely postponing the refugees and riots he dreads. My own dread is that of my Muslim friend. I can see how, at some time, these forty million may choose religious loyalty over national loyalty and fulfill the prediction of Hindu nationalists and fanatics by serving as a Pakistani fifth column.

The leader refuses to take my remarks seriously. "You have to put on more fat before you can hold weighty opinions like these," he says. "Don't mistake me," he adds gently. "I'm not anti-Muslim. If anything, I am too pro-Muslim."

I stop him there and ask if this isn't the very thing of which the Muslims complain. No one, I say, likes to be treated with patronizing indulgence.

"You can't have it both ways," he says. "You can't claim a privileged position and at the same time blame the government for giving you the privileges. There are many difficulties. All we can do is let sleeping dogs lie—sit on the issues."

But are Indian Muslims really asking for a privileged position? Or are we being indulgent because we are afraid of them? How can the secular state survive when we have separate laws for different religious groups—when we legislate that Hindus must be monogamous and Muslims need not be? The Sikhs and untouchables ask for privileges equal to those of the Muslims. The Muslims are uneasy because of their privileges. And the leaders sit on the issues.

"What else is there to do?" he says. "This is our heritage from the past." India is a country of many races, languages, and religions, he goes on. Placate one religious minority or language group, and all the others will make demands. There are so many empty stomachs here that any cause can get a following. There is only one historical parallel to our situation—the Austro-Hungarian empire, which, like India, enclosed many minorities. It collapsed, leaving behind it splinter states from which rose ruthless dictators. The fanatics in our country who want an autonomous Dravidian state and those who want a separate Sikh state and those who would like the country to be partitioned according to language do not realize these dangers. The states would simply fall as prizes to dictators, who would fight among themselves, because their countries would not be economically viable. But how can you read history books to fanatics? It is almost entirely because of the Prime Minister that India is one nation. If the Prime Minister lives for some time, and if there is no war between Pakistan and India, we may still be able, by enlightened policy, to develop national loyalties. "But," he admonishes, "you go along and have some words with our military people. Wander through the bureaucracy and see our problems. We've only touched on a few of them."

His A.D.C. rings up a military chief, and a few hours later I

am conversing with the military people. I find myself in a building with secret chambers and shut doors, and while I am waiting
for the chief I chat with his A.D.C. (India has as many A.D.C.s
as America has secretaries, and, like the secretaries, the A.D.C.s
really run the country.) I ask the A.D.C. what the cloak-and-
dagger atmosphere indicates. "We have here a system of inter-
cepting messages and breaking codes," he says. "There are
strange inefficiencies in Pakistan. Just the other day, there was a
broadcast from Karachi to the Pakistani formations in Kashmir
directing them to change their position. The Pakistani signal
operator shouted the coded message repeatedly, but the reception was bad and the man at the receiving end didn't seem to
understand very much. Finally, the signal operator blurted out,
'You mother sleeping sister sleeping! Can't you understand?
I'm telling you to move the formations from —— to ——.' This
is how we break the code. These Pakistani Muslims really lack
control. They'll never learn, and we'll always be one jump ahead
of them."

"You know," I say sententiously, "today Europe would be
Muslim if it hadn't been for Charles Martel in 732."

"What did you say?" he says.

"Today Europe would be Muslim if it hadn't been for Charles
Martel in 732."

"What does that have to do with Kashmir?"

At that moment, a shut door opens and I am led in to the chief.
He sits down on a big sofa and talks about the dangers of military dictatorship. Pakistan, he tells me, is a military dictatorship,
but India is different, because the national Army is devoted to
Nehru's government. But the danger is always there; the officers,
at present devoid of political ambition, may acquire it. Am I
aware that there is some conflict between the political and military high commands at this moment? In the Army, promotion
by merit is everything. When a private joins the Army, he knows
the exact ratio of the ranks—so many privates to so many corporals, so many corporals to so many sergeants, and on up the
ladder—and he calculates his chances of higher pay and rank
accordingly. If a politician takes it into his head to promote this

favorite or that, even if it's only one or two, the Army as an organization is shattered. The faith of the private in his future is shattered. This is probably the story behind General Thimayya's protest resignation. If the Defense Minister, Krishna Menon, had been playing political favorites, General Thimayya had good reason for his resignation. He was forced to retract his resignation, because a democracy like ours cannot afford a truculent Army, however just its grievances. Both the military and the politicians seem confused about what the relation between them is to be, and whether the military can be left as an autonomous power with the potential of upsetting the government. The main thing to remember is that India is surrounded by what might be called military dictatorships. Ceylon, Indonesia, and Pakistan have all been taken over by dictators. China presses from the north, Pakistan from the east and west, and we are left to defend ourselves with weapons purchased abroad. The chief challenges me : " Has any nation ever successfully fought a war with bought weapons? The real defenses of a country are its industrial potential. Our industrial power is slight, and we are faced with the two biggest enemies in the world. A war with Pakistan could enlist the resources and sympathies of the Islamic world, a war with China those of the Communist world. What would we have to draw upon? Obsolete weapons stamped 'Made in England.' "

" What do you plan to do about it?" I ask.

" Nothing." Just sit on the issues. That's all you can do in India—sit on the issues. Put on a front—feel big, act big, and think big.

I leave the grave chief sitting on his sofa, and go to the Planning Commission to find out how the economic theoreticians are going to reshape the country. I glean statistics and pore over pamphlets and plans. I learn that there can be no comparison between the India of 1947 and the Russia of 1917. India has nearly twice the population of Russia and one-sixth the land to support it. Our country is excellent for growing grain and fruit. It has coal and iron and manganese and mica for large industries. But the population is rising too fast, at the rate of seven million people more a year, and the problems of providing housing, food, and education for these successive seven millions are stupendous.

The Deputy Chairman of the Commission, Mr. V. T. Krishnamachari, explains that when figures get into millions they stop meaning anything. He tries to make me visualize half a million children born every month and his task of providing a place in society for them. As for birth control, the present methods are too messy, too expensive. India must also sit on the population issue.

Krishnamachari is angered when Western reporters call his five-year plans too ambitious. "Our present per-capita income is sixty dollars a year, and by 1975 we hope to have it up to a hundred and twenty dollars a year," he says. "Is this ambition?" He thinks that the Western reporters have been far too enthusiastic about China's progress. He works continuously with facts and statistics, and knows how they can be manipulated to support any conclusion. Until 1954, Chinese economists were working on a false economic principle: "The more people, the better the country." Since then, the economists have reversed themselves, but their false principle must have cost the Chinese something. Everyone knows that dictatorial methods are speedy, and the Chinese have proved this by their campaign against "enemy fly" and "enemy sparrow." But a complete transformation of the economy from agrarian to industrial or from poor to rich takes time in either a dictatorship or a democracy.

India's race with China is very important, and the outcome will be touch and go. The victory of China is by no means a foregone conclusion, as some of the nervous reporters in the West believe. In his learned way, the Deputy Chairman sneers at Western reporters for their jargon: "P-bomb" for rising population. Such jargon simply makes people jittery. "We are not children that we have to remember things with alphabets." A for Apple concludes the interview.

Formal interviews end in the face of a present crisis in the state of Kerala. Kerala is in many ways unique among the states of India: The only elected Communist government. A high level of literacy; almost sixty per cent of its people read and write, while in the rest of the country from twenty to twenty-five per cent is the average. The only state predominantly Christian; instead of Hindu and Muslim, a strong Catholic hierarchy. The Communists were elected by an uneasy alliance with Christians, then turned on their allies and tried to make convent education Marxist. Communists and Catholics ran afoul of each other, violence erupted in the streets, prisons overflowed with Christians, and the central government finally stepped in to depose the state government.

I go to the lower house of Parliament, the House of the People, to hear the debate on Kerala. Communist members shout excitedly. Democracy is dead in India. All elections are a farce if a government can be deposed willy-nilly.

Prime Minister Nehru speaks for endless hours; unruffled by interruptions and jeers, he defends the action of the central government. Sometimes people break out into laughter, and sometimes their faces are red with rage. Sometimes the air-conditioners go off. Sometimes, as in the bazaars, people shout at each other. The habit of shouting seems Indian, not Anglo-Saxon, and I feel as if I were out on the Indian streets instead of in the House of the People. The Prime Minister argues his case like a lawyer, patiently outlining the disturbances in Kerala, the misuse of power by the Communist government, the debates of his Cabinet, his conferences with the Communist leaders, and his prolonged but futile attempts to reach a solution without the intervention of the central government. He speaks from notes and seems to address the nation as well as the Parliament. His decision is not that of a dictator but that of a responsible governor. The methods of the Communists threaten democracy. I leave the debate with a lively sense of democracy in action in India. India cannot sit on the issues when democracy is threatened.

Jayaprakash Narayan comes to Delhi, and the journalists arrange a tea for him. When I left India, after Independence, he was the leader of the younger generation, the theorist of the Socialist Party, and an intellectual rival of the Prime Minister, listened to respectfully at home and abroad. The Prime Minister himself courted him for a time. Narayan's followers, who saw him as the probable successor to Nehru, were disappointed when he left politics to follow Vinoba Bhave, a new Gandhi, who walks from village to village collecting gifts of land from the landowners for redistribution to the landless. I remember Narayan as the politician rather than the saint. The journalists of the leading newspapers—the *Statesman,* the *Times of India,* the *Hindustan Times,* and the *Indian Express*—pick Narayan's brains. They sip their tea and prepare their editorials. Narayan commends the action of the central government in Kerala. Kerala, he says, is a laboratory experiment of Communist strategy. The Communists will use constitutional means to grasp power, but once they have power they will abuse it. What they did in Kerala is a good lesson for the masses; we have reason to be pleased. Frank Moraes, editor of the *Indian Express,* explains to me that Narayan's remarks on Kerala are significant because of his political disinterestedness and his sainthood in the eyes of the people.

From Kerala the journalists press on to the threat of China. They recall that Narayan was one of the first Indians to respond with feeling to the plight of the Dalai Lama. When the god of the Tibetan Buddhists fled his country and asked for a home in India for himself and his party, the government seemed embarrassed. What was to happen to the friendship of India and China, to amicable relations between the two countries? (Moraes explains to me that the Prime Minister has not always been deluded by the tinsel promises of the peace-loving Chinese. Ten years ago, Moraes was asked to go on a cultural mission to China. The Prime Minister took the delegates aside to say that China threatened not only the borders of India but the spine of Asia. If the Prime Minister has been inactive, either he has miscalculated the time when the Chinese could safely act on their hidden intentions or he has felt helpless and has tried to prolong India's neutrality as far as possible in order to transform the country. He may also have been deluded by some of his advisers into a wrong evaluation of the Chinese threat.) Narayan admits to uncertainty about the Dalai Lama and China. He wonders what Nehru would have done if he had been an exile during the Indian Nationalist struggle and had been greeted with the chill reception accorded the Dalai Lama. While Narayan is distressed by the Prime Minister's prudent calculations, he realizes that the Chinese threat is paralyzing, and that, whatever the differences between him and Mr. Nehru, India has little choice but to sit and wait. India and China should go to the conference table. India and China should try to reach new border agreements. India should be prepared to establish a Himalayan federation if that is the choice of the Himalayan peoples. "We cannot apply double standards in our foreign policy," he says. "We cannot protest on behalf of ruled colonies if we appear to create our own Himalayan protectorates in Nepal, Sikkim, and Bhutan."

We must sit and wait, but I find Narayan's posture uncomfortable. For a decade, India has been self-appointed moral tutor to the world. She kept alive the cause of China, she lashed out on Suez, but she held her tongue on Hungary until it was too late. She harangued the world about idealism and about the evils of diplomacy based on *Realpolitik*. And all this time she had a skeleton in her cupboard. She was taking one stand on China in public but privately harboring quite a different view of her. If we must sit and wait, we can be more comfortably propped up by admitting our loyalties to the West. However great our size, we are helpless alone.

Narayan appears more and more uncomfortable as the discussion turns on politics and power. He moves to the saintlier ground of the *bhudan* movement and delivers a sermon. Technology is as much a matter of the spirit as of invention. Technology must be humanized, and the land-gift movement is the road to humanized technology. Gandhi had his face set against making India an industrial society. In his view, the way to a new India was through village-home industry and village democracy, through a sense of pride in work, a sense of belonging to a community of work. *Bhudan* is Gandhi's spirit in action—the lectures, the hymns, the marches, the meetings, the quiet exhortations to the assembled landowners, and the voluntary gifts of millions and millions of acres. Narayan warms to his theme.

D

Vinoba Bhave is working in Gandhi's tradition—a tradition of spiritual socialism, which is to be the great gift of India to political thought. *Bhudan* is not utopian; it is a revolution at the grass roots, and Indian, rather than Western, in origin. "You can see the power of our new socialism when you talk to the landowners about giving up some of their land to the landless peasants, and appeal to the good in them," Narayan says, with soft pride. He admits that the land proffered may be barren, may be in strips and therefore impractical for cultivation, but he argues that the movement is important in its tangible reckonings as well as in its spiritual power. I come away feeling the loss of Narayan the politician to Narayan the saint but with the conviction that in India there may be more progress through spiritual appeal than through political legislation. In Narayan's own words, "land reform is as much a matter of conscience as a matter of legislation, and conscience can be aroused only by appealing to the good in us." This is Gandhi's India, the India of the Ganges, the India of the ages, and Narayan is the real son of his country.

I walk out from the tea writing my own editorial, "Past and Present," but I don't think it would be publishable in many Indian papers. There are not enough Narayans in India, I write. Older men, including the President, talk day in and day out of the degeneration of the Indian character since independence, of the growth of crime, poverty, and hunger. They deplore the deterioration of politics in Free India, not so much in the central government as in the fourteen states established by the federal Constitution. In these states, political offices are sometimes gained through the greasing of peasant palms. The politicians, when elected, use their offices to build an empire for their families and friends. Not many can afford disinterested action; they must instead cushion themselves against their return to the poverty of private life. An entire class of political entrepreneurs is emerging. In a country with little economic security, with high unemployment for men and hardly any employment for women, family is often put above national interest. Can liberal democracy survive in such a country? This is my question and this is my lament. The list of India's difficulties is endless.

If one is not a saint, one must grow callous to the life around one and wander through India tongueless, with eyes shut, eardrums punctured, I write. One must follow the example of the three wise monkeys—speak not, see not, hear not. Problems are too many and solutions too few. But man is not a monkey. With his reason and his sensibilities, he must speak out or burst from the strain of keeping silence. There is a terrible lack of urgency in India. Most of the books I have read about India miss the mark. They are either too optimistic or too pessimistic about her future, and I think optimism is more dangerous than pessimism. If everyone keeps on talking about India with sympathetic optimism, we may be deluded long enough to permit democracy to slip away from us, and soft-pedal ourselves into disaster. If the Indian democracy is to survive, we must separate history from prejudice. We can never wish away the British raj. We can, but we should not, load on a British scapegoat our divisions and our shortcomings. Our history is both Indian and British. We must commend the British for their Civil Service, for their law and order, and for giving our country at least a semblance of unity. We must commend the British for teaching us their language. Instead of ruling us as the Dutch ruled the Indonesians—Dutch officers did not share even language with their clerks—our rulers introduced us to the literature of revolt. It was a rare thing for an Indian educated under English masters not to be exposed, at one time or another, to John Stuart Mill's essay "On Liberty." We acquired as political saints Milton, Mill, and Shaw, and while the object of the British in educating us may have been nothing more than to staff the Civil Service with clerks, by their decision to teach these clerks English they extended to us a privilege—one whose consequences they could not completely foresee. Now, free from the British raj, we must at least thank them for this.

With these gains recognized, I write, we can more justly assess our losses. As a sub-continent, India was ruled by a few thousand Englishmen and her history reduced to a subtopic in the chronicle of British imperialism. The English robbed us of a sense of history. We looked to our past in a spirit of ancestor worship and became indifferent to our present. In this heap of broken history, we lost our identity. In 1947, with Independence, the present became our own. But some people continue to prefer fancy to history. It is fanciful to think that the British raj could have been prolonged to our advantage. A country cannot be made ready for freedom by her rulers; she must go it alone. It is fanciful to think that our unity could have been won through violent revolution. Hungary showed that where a state commands modern means of destruction, violent revolution must fail. Revolution as a concept is out dated. Even if violent revolution had been possible, it is even more fanciful to think that struggle would have kept India united. Though the British fostered division, they did not create it. Present movements to repartition the country on religious and linguistic lines demonstrate the disunity cleaving India. No, fancy is pleasant but history remains. India is her history—independent, struggling, and disunited.

Present-day India must be a compromise, I write. Peaceful revolution left us with British formulas. We avoided a violent break with the past, and so were deprived of the utopian energy of other revolutions. But we had a choice : to improve boldly on the old formulas or to apply them slavishly to problems too large for them. In drafting a Constitution, we audaciously revised them to our needs—a federal state within the Commonwealth. But in clinging to a Civil Service more British than Indian, for example, we propped up our new country with dead history. In compromise India, the old Indian Civil Service goes on. The prestige and power of the Civil Service in India are almost unrivalled in the free world. Its system is British-born—admission by competition, promotion as a result of tact and seniority— and its life reflects the feeble ideal of a public school in Victorian England. First, the best minds are bought for the Civil Service, then they are reduced to a uniform talent. A public-school boy must be good not only at cricket and classics but at obedience. A first secretary, if he is so ordered, should be able to clean the secretariat better than the charwoman. Only through unquestioning obedience can command be learned. The Civil Service is run like a military organization. Orders issued at any level must be obeyed by those below. Deference must be adjusted to the chain of command and everyone must know his station. The wife of a second secretary should cultivate the wife of No. 1 and be condescending toward the wife of No. 3. Empty conventions provide the pomp indispensable to the system. Carbon copies and files almost outnumber people; only the carbons and the files are considered irreplaceable. Conventions, rules, precedents can never be waived. One exception will establish a rule and bind the Civil Service forever.

I write that the English perpetrated this rigid system for their clerks, not for themselves. But these Indian clerks, who are now officers, carry on the repressive tradition of Victorian England. They fear to speak their mind lest they jeopardize their promotion. No wonder many officers enjoy more their posts in the districts than promotion in the secretariat; in the districts they are at least in touch with people and problems. Dispensing justice in individual cases, gathering statistics about a flood or a famine, delving into local records and working with them like historians, advising on the collection of taxes—all these are much more invigorating than sitting in Delhi. Decorum, the right degree of deference for officers, and a rigid concept of rulers and ruled remain the tenets of our new administrative service, while the Civil Services of other nations are abandoning them. There are great and conspicuous exceptions to the Civil Service establishment—N. Raghavan Pillai, Secretary-General of the Ministry of External Affairs, is one of them—but these exceptions are few. Unlike their English predecessors, many of the officers lack confidence and are afraid to make an authoritative decision without referring the matter to their superiors. Responsibilities pass from hand to hand until someone has the courage to forget them. Often the Prime Minister is forced to be his own Civil Service. Little squabbles—a personal problem of this officer and that—are all appealed to him. Despite its boasted efficiency, the Civil Service sits on the issues. For many years, it will remain the preferred career of ambitious young men and women in India, because in an economically insecure country government employment offers the only security. If we shrink from experiment and refuse to depart from old conventions, we may find ourselves reduced to carbon copies of the British raj. The Civil Service, like so many things in India, is a holdover from the tarnished glories of the British raj. We find it hard to live with, harder to live without. Our choice is to live with fake standards or to live with no standards at all, which is almost to say that choice does not exist.

The absence of choice is the Indian blind alley of analysis, of intelligence, I write. I come up against a granite wall of problems, but this does not prevent me from having opinions and ideas. I disagree with the weak policy of Nehru's government toward China. I wish that in our diplomacy we were less philosophical and more realistic; that if we really were aware of the Chinese threat earlier, we had abandoned our isolationist policy, at least in part, and sought assistance from the Western powers. I regret our fighting for a Pyrrhic victory in Kashmir. I differ with the government's underplaying of the religious issue, which seems to gloss over the real problem of the Muslim minority and simply postpone the threat to the secular state. Indeed, I object to the too conciliatory policy toward minorities, whether religious or linguistic. I abhor the attachment of second-class politicians to the Prime Minister's person, and his loyalty to his friends, who sometimes abuse his trust with impunity. (This tolerance, while a very commendable personal trait, cannot be thought politically astute.) I am impatient with his government for its small progress toward breaking down the caste barriers, for its failure to inject more creativity into the Civil Service. I even take exception to the federal Constitution, which created as many legislatures and Chief Ministers as states instead of a sensibly unified government for the nation. And, however justified the reasons for it, I am saddened, I write, by the dearth of a younger generation of leaders. The Gandhian way is attractive but thorny. The English path is indulgent but, for the Indians, sterile.

3

INDIAN SUMMER

Before spending a bummy month together in India, Dom Moraes and I were great friends at Oxford. I am not quite sure what friendship means elsewhere, but at Oxford it means being able to spend a whole day together—that is, from breakfast to bed-time—and being able to roam from room to room, sometimes bumming drinks, sometimes taking along hip flasks and sharing drinks with other friends. At Oxford, we worked frightfully hard perhaps for five or six days, five or six weeks, and after this intensive period we took a physical and spiritual holiday, bum-ming and being amiable, visiting and being visited. These bummy days were an Oxford specialty. Just as some people have Sabbath days, we had bummy days. They are necessary to those of us who lead serious lives day in and day out, like ants on the pages of a folio musty with age and use. But these were not so much days of rest as days of motion, days of looking out on life through whiskey-colored glasses, days when we spent most of our time pacing, just so we would remember how to use our legs and feet.

Both Dom and I graduated from Oxford in July, and perhaps, before I get too deeply occupied with other matters, it would be best to say a word or two about the literary set to which Dom and I belonged at Oxford. In contrast to the smart set, our literary set was always changing, like the water in the river. Sometimes it included people like a boy I'll call Elton, who, after graduating, was engaged in half-hearted research—and research at Oxford amounts to very little, especially if you have had a book or two of poems published by a respectable press. Elton was happily engaged to a very pretty girl until he unhappily discovered he was a homosexual. Sometimes our set included people like Del, who had received first-class honors in English and could therefore live off the capital of his brilliant under-graduate career. Del, although an American from the Middle West and a Midwestern university, was more English in manner and accent than most Englishmen from the South of England. Sometimes it included people like Patrick, a talented actor and an Oxford figure; sometimes it was visited by the three boys who ran the literary magazines at the university; and sometimes Jasper, a great classic at Balliol, would join us to sneer at the last piece of clever, clever writing in *Isis*. The set did have certain constant features, such as the mistresses of the littérateurs, but otherwise it was always in a state of flux. So, you see, it wasn't really a set. It was just a river of people. Because of the very nature of the river, our customs were not fixed—except, that is, between two or three friends.

Dom Moraes—like me, an Indian—was much more idle than I, but then he was a poet. He didn't have to worry about degrees, and that kind of thing. A small book of poems of his, "A Begin-ning," had been a triumphant success. His poetry was highly personal, sensuous, and filled with what one critic termed "rap-turous ironies." He wrote like Dylan Thomas, he was lovable like Thomas, and, like Thomas, he was a ladies' man. In our talk, Dom and I often attached "kins" to words. We liked the words better that way. Perhaps it was a remnant of pig Latin, but we thought of it as, somehow, Socratic. Of course, we couldn't really explain it at all. When we were both drunk (Domkins more than mekins), we attached "kins" to practically everything. It was just more bummy and more comradely. We also had a habit of putting "little" and "tiny" in front of words. For example, one of us might say to the other, "Let us go and see our little friend," or "Let us go and see our tiny friend." Now, "little friend" and "tiny friend" most of the time, though not always, referred to young ladies, but we called them "little friend" and "tiny friend" not because they were Lolitas but simply because the words "little" and "tiny" gave, we thought, more rhythm to our speech and, anyway, made it characteristically our own, as opposed to everyone else's. There were many other nuances of speech and habit in our friendship. For instance, we seldom told an unvarnished truth; we made whatever happened to us more fanciful and funny, to amuse ourselves and our friends. (In this Dom was more gifted than I, but he brought out my playful self.) This was not necessarily intentional. It was just part of our natures, or perhaps, more accurately, it was an escape from our natures. Both of us wore heavy armor, and our nonsense shielded us from the public, and from each other, and from ourselves. This is, in fact, to say that the friendship between Dom and me was English—reserved, witty, sarcastic, intellectual, and sometimes uncommunicative, if you took words alone as an index of feelings. But perhaps I've said enough to give some hint of the background to our month in India.

I arrive in New Delhi in the middle of July—sunstroke, heat, flies, and starving millions. I have been away from India for ten years, living in America and England. I spend some weeks getting reacquainted with the country and my family. I visit villages, I call on politicians and religious leaders, I lunch with the Prime Minister, I talk with strangers on the street. This, I am told, is part of my education; it is very necessary—in fact, morally obligatory. I am saddened by the unhappiness around me. It is overwhelming; I and everyone say that this is because I am unable to keep my wits about me, have been away so long. Everyone advises a furlough. I think of it more as a bummy period. Just then, the telephone rings and penetrates the educative process. "This is me!" says a voice. "Hello, it's you, on the phonekins," I reply, and Oxford is in India. Adolescence all over again. Fun all over again. Dom, who has come to New Delhi with his father, has spent some weeks in Bombay doing much the same thing I have been doing, so he, too, needs a furlough. He settles into a room in a posh hotel, and fills the cabinet with nectar—drinks for him and tiny drinks for me. We get together— a bummy Oxford surprise. First thing we do after some drinking is to go to the Volga, a bourgeois Delhi place with upper-class pretensions. Dom is slightly unmanageable. I order a four-course dinner. Dom says he wants nothing to eat, but I say he must eat, because liquids without solids are bad for the health. So I order for him. Dom speaks only English, for though he was brought up in Bombay, he's had much less Indian background than I. I am at home in three Indian languages and so can order conveniently. Dom accidentally splashes soup on my suit, then feeds a tiny bit of rice to imaginary dogs under the table. I am embarrassed but enjoy being the center of attention. A Sikh at the far-left table picks up the phone, dials a number, then tries, in Punjabi, to persuade someone to come to the Volga immediately. "You can't imagine what is going on here," he says. "Just come for five minutes." (The fool doesn't realize that I can understand Punjabi.) Dom then feeds a tiny bit of pudding to the imaginary dogs. The waiters don't know what to do. The orchestra starts playing conservative English melodies as loudly and furiously as possible. We stagger out, to everyone's relief, and get a taxi and order the driver to take us to my home.

Dom tries to give his whole bankroll to the taxi-driver for his kind services. The taxi-driver thanks him profusely, but I insist that Dom doesn't really want to do this. "But I do," he says, and the taxi-driver believes him. I intervene, and save the money and the situation by taking Dom into the house.

Next morning, Dom is up early. "Bad influence of gin," he says. "Scotch is much better, gives you longer sleep." I breakfast, but Dom does not. We explain to the family that he is not hungry.

We wander out into the streets, and are soon choking with dust, heat, and lack of direction. Who are the great literary people in Delhi? We cannot think of many. We head for the house of Khushwant Singh, a Sikh novelist and translator of English. We catch him unawares—nothing on his head, and his hair covering his face—but he hides his surprise and expresses his delight. His thick, long hair makes him look like a scarecrow from the back. He puts on a turban and seems at once genuinely pleased to see us. He wants to do an article on Dom, make him better known in India. We discuss the possibilities for a great Indian novel. Both Dom and I make fatuous remarks, but Khushwant says it is possible to have a great Indian novel in English. We heckle him, and he adores it. We think he's wonderful: large and tall; lecherous eyes; open face and open humor; beard covering his Adam's apple. He talks a colloquial Punjabi, like a villager just come to town. But as soon as he speaks English he becomes a sophisticate at St. James's.

From Khushwant's we go to Narayana Menon's. Menon is magnificent: tall and lean; bright eyes; pipe; wonderfully long, delicate fingers; manners like Del's; five years' experience at the B.B.C.; a book on Yeats; the sensibilities and responsiveness of a musician. He plays us a beautiful southern melody on an Indian instrument. He plucks it lovingly. There is something very artistic about the atmosphere—wicker chairs, great paintings by Hussain and Jamini Roy on the walls, the room filled with books —and his little daughter wants autographs. We thumb through the pages of her autograph book. The book seems to include the signatures of all the great writers who have visited India in the last five years, plus those of all the Indian painters. Narayana says he left the B.B.C., on a wave of enthusiasm for Independence, to join All India Radio, and now thinks it was a great mistake. Bureaucracy is immobile and trying, and does not allow him to do creative programs, such as he could do on the Third. He is robbed of English happiness. Narayana becomes our mentor. All of a sudden, Delhi begins to smile. The heat is no longer like kilns but like animals. We drink beer in mugs; after each fill we say " Cheers," and we talk of Michelangelo and Yehudi Menuhin and Oxford. It seems we are smoking the fag end of an Oxford cigarette.

That afternoon, Dom and I accept an invitation to go to All India Radio. Dom plays hard to get. Says he's leaving for Russia tomorrow. If they want him to read his poems, he must have the studio that very minute. He throws the whole machine out of gear. The All India Radio people are eager to have both of us interviewed, but we can't think of a subject. We want to chat and gossip. They wish for something more definite. They ask us whether we want to be interviewed by somebody. So we have the director ring up Khushwant. Khushwant is sleeping, but we have him awakened. He says he won't come in a taxi, even though the director will pay the cost. He wants a special All India limousine sent for him. Some more telephoning, and a V.I.P. limousine goes for Khushwant. We get a studio and perform individually, and then Khushwant interviews us. Then some more discussions, and quarrels with the director. But, strangely, by the end of the afternoon they like us. They cannot say why; perhaps it's because we are different. We come away from All India Radio pleased with ourselves. It is evening.

Evenings are a problem in Delhi, so we ask the taxi-driver about "entertainment." He giggles maliciously, looks back at our faces and clothes, and then removes the evil smirk from his face. "The best night club is in that hotel around the corner," he says.

"Can we drink there?" Dom asks.

"There is no drink and no cabaret in Delhi—that is, in public," the taxi-driver says.

"What shall we do there?" I ask, and the smirk returns.

We discover he's a pimp. "If you really want to hear some singing and see some good dancing . . ."

I understand, but Dom does not, because, as I've said, he was brought up in a very English atmosphere (his father is from Goa and is an Oxford graduate) and can't speak a word of any native language. He thinks this a good thing, because he writes his poetry in English. I tell Dom about the driver's suggestion. He breaks into a long laugh, and I really think the driver is hurt, or perhaps believes he has made a mistake, because he says nothing more. We go on to Dom's room, and I have a drink and he has drinks. But there's still nothing to do, so we wander out again and go to the very posh Gymkhana Club. It's like walking into the house of the Viceroy himself; one sees his ghost stamping up and down. The club has one of the few real bars in Delhi, and the Kashmir Room, and a large, sumptuous, brocaded dining room, where the orchestra plays light, frothy music, and

where Indian husbands dance with wives, now and again shouting "Whoopee!" in what they think is an American way. Little
children of the civil servants swim in the swimming pool, and
there are almost more bearers than members.

When we walk into the club, the head porter can hardly
understand what we say. "I never heard anyone talk so softly!
Aren't they well mannered?" he shouts behind us as we begin
our tour of the shadow of the British raj. (By now, Dom and I
have decided to tour our country like wandering minstrels, reading poetry and talking.) And by and by we come upon both our
fathers, and they introduce us to two sisters and their mother.
These are delicious girls. They seem to be just out of the health
shop—pink all over, liquid eyes—and they speak English as
though they'd just come from England, though they are wearing
saris. I notice that they also speak English to the bearers, and
the bearers are impressed. They have unpronounceable names.
It's hard to hear because of the noise, so Dom and I whisper to
each other, referring to our new acquaintances as "the pink
girls." Their mother is constantly pushing them forward, until
the girls are on top of us.

They are terribly well shaped and pretty, but we can't deter-
mine their ages. They seem eager, and we feel a bit hemmed in,
and try to disappear, but we don't succeed until we have been
forced to accept an invitation to tea at their home in the old
city the next day.

We go back to Dom's hotel, drink some more, and have an
enormous meal brought up to the room. We eat it very hastily
and nervously, because the bearers, who won't go out of the
room, stare at us. We feel guilty, and we look out of the window,
and there is somebody scrounging in the dustbins. "Ved," Dom
says, "what is that line in 'Howl'—'The best minds of my
generation . . . dragging themselves through the negro streets'?"
We feel terribly depressed, and I have another drink and Dom
has some more drinks. Then we start gossiping about Khushwant,
the radio, and the pink girls. We note that the pinks would be
good for bedkins. We note that they are different from other
Indian girls in saris, who are shy and blush too easily, without

cause. We think their mother is terribly sweet but a bit too aggressive. All in all, we are troubled about the pinks.

Next day brings good news: A visitor from abroad, a Canadian reporter, is in India. We are introduced to him at breakfast by a common acquaintance. He is dressed with an Edwardian elegance suitable for a morning call at court, but his paunch, twice the size of any other in the middle-class, middle-aged world, destroys the lines of his suit. His complexion is sallow, he's stubby, and he looks every bit of his early forties. In our short-hand Dom and I call him the Canadian mahatma; he was Gandhi's acquaintance and has written about himself and the Mahatma.

I must have copy ready for the *Statesman,* so I rush away, leaving the Canadian mahatma in Dom's charge. When I return to Dom's room for morning coffee, he tells me that after breakfast he and the Canadian mahatma went to Gandhi's grave. The mahatma, who had already started drinking, looked at the grass and the trees and said, "Where is the loincloth? Bring on the loincloth!" The pilgrims stared at him, unable to understand why an expensively dressed Canadian, bottle in hand, should require a loincloth. Taking out a large silk handkerchief, the Canadian mahatma spread it on the grass. Dom found the performance eccentric and un-understandable. The mahatma, straightening his suit, sat on his handkerchief and wept drunken tears. And then he ceremoniously stood up, leaving his improvised loincloth on the ground.

Dom continues, "We returned to the hotel, and he forced me to recite some poems and he wept some more. I've never seen anything like it. I couldn't very well ask him why he was weeping, but after one of the poems he said, 'The Mahatma would have wept, because the Mahatma liked Beauty, and I have been left the custodian of Beauty.'"

"What is all this nonsense?" I say to Dom. "You mistake me for one of your audiences."

While we are talking, the telephone rings and the Canadian mahatma asks us to come and help him pack. He is leaving that afternoon. Before we know it, Dom and I are in a taxi going to his hotel. It is a new, fashionable hotel, one of the most expensive hotels in Delhi. It is mainly for foreigners. It would cost the average Indian a year's income to live there a week.

We take the lift and walk through a labyrinth to reach his door. The Canadian mahatma has a bottle of whiskey in each hand.

"Have a drink," he says, and we sit down. I refuse the drink. It is only eleven-thirty in the morning.

"Shouldn't we pack first?" I ask.

"No, sit down," the Canadian mahatma says. He looks better sitting down in a chair, because the paunch is less obtrusive when it is doubled up.

"I wonder if the Mahatma would have liked this nonsense," I whisper to Dom. Dom clears his throat uncomfortably. "You know," I continue aloud, "the Mahatma used to live on three and a half annas a day."

The Canadian mahatma looks hurt and explains defensively, "It wasn't always easy to find refrigeration in primitive villages. Some days, Ghandhi's simple meal used to cost a couple of dollars to produce. When he was in England, goat's milk was a positive luxury."

The Canadian mahatma seems to be using dirty words in a temple. Dom clears his throat uncomfortably again. He isn't saying very much, so I have to ask the questions. "What time is your plane?"

"We must lie down and think," the Canadian mahatma says.

I repeat the question.

"We must lie down and think."

The bearer comes in with some nuts. "Sahib, your plane leaves at two, and last night your friend asked me to tell you that you should leave the hotel by one."

The Canadian mahatma yawns and asks for more ice.

"Perhaps, sir, we ought to help you pack," Dom says.

"The Mahatma was the greatest saint since Buddha," says the Canadian mahatma. "Gandhiji comprehended the great Indian truth—that one must either be a politician or a saint. He was both, but I am neither. I am just a writer." He stops, thinks, continues, "I must lie down and think—that is what the Mahatma would have done if he had been corrupt, like me."

I am exasperated. It is already twelve-fifteen. "May I call the bearer?" I ask. "He could pack for you."

The Canadian mahatma shakes his big head vigorously. "Don't you dare do that," he says. I disregard the drunken injunction. I ring for the bearer, and he comes. He is a tall, thin man dressed in the uniform of the hotel—white turban, long white coat with white belt, white drill trousers, white tennis shoes. His belt buckle is the hotel's initial on a brass plate. He has a big cloth over his arm. His manner is deferential. I speak to him in Hindi. "Don't pay any attention to the sahib. Fetch the suitcase and bring out the clothes."

Ridiculous activity. The bearer drags out an old suitcase tied with hemp, and the Canadian mahatma tries to make him put it back. I tell the bearer to get the clothes. The bearer shuttles from one sahib to the other, but I win and the Canadian mahatma seems reconciled.

Piles of clothes dwarf the suitcase. We look for another. The Canadian mahatma shouts, "There is no other! Gandhiji carried only one sack, I carry only one suitcase!" I translate this for the bearer.

The bearer inquires how the sahib got all the clothes into the hotel. A good question, I think, and I put it to the Canadian mahatma.

"I wore them on my back—can't you see I'm a rich bastard who likes to show his clothes?"

I leave the bearer in his ignorance.

The Canadian mahatma fingers the piles of clothing, turns over replicas of the suit he is wearing, silk shirts with French cuffs and detachable collars, several dressing gowns. He asks the bearer, through me, if he wants some clothes. The answer is yes.

"Here, can you use a silk dressing gown?"

"No, Sahib, but my wife would wear it in the bazaars and bless you."

The Canadian mahatma tosses the dressing gown to the bearer.

"Shirts?"

"Yes, Sahib."

Half a dozen silk shirts join the dressing gown on the floor.

The action continues. The bearer, like a vender, now sits in front of the suitcase. To his left is the Canadian mahatma's diminishing pile, to his right a steadily growing one—his own. He hugs it, and his face recalls the monkey in a story I knew as a child. Two cats fight over a fish, and the monkey, chosen to divide it fairly, gobbles it all. Where are the cats?

"Ask the bearer what he would do if he had all these clothes," the Canadian mahatma tells me.

I ask, and the bearer says, "I would give a suit to each of my brothers. We would have a feast on the sahib's birthday and pray for him."

"How in hell do you know when my birthday is? Anyway, I'm not worthy."

I edit his answer.

"If you like, we will wear them on Christmas."

"Is this man a Christian?" The question is directed to me.

Yes, the bearer is a Christian convert. His whole village, in the United Province, follows Jesus Christ. The Canadian mahatma is really angry. "Converts have no ethics. They have been corrupted. I didn't come to India to give clothes to Christians. I must lie down and think."

Translation becomes difficult. I cannot convey the hurt of the Canadian mahatma to the bearer or the confusion of the bearer to the Canadian mahatma.

"Damn. Wear them—wear them on Gandhiji's birthday. Or Nehru's birthday. Look—will you swear to wear them on Nehru's birthday?"

The bearer swears. But when the Canadian mahatma presses him for Nehru's birth date he becomes evasive, and finally takes refuge behind drawn-out calculations involving the Hindu calendar. He arrives at the right day and is rewarded with a dinner jacket.

E

"Wear it and let me see how it looks on you."

The bearer is embarrassed. He holds the dazzling dinner jacket in his cloth without touching it.

"He must put it on," commands the Canadian mahatma.

I prod the bearer. Finally, we force him into the bathroom with the dinner jacket.

"It will be too loose for him."

"But you won't take it back, will you?" It occurs to me that this may be the Canadian mahatma's way of jesting, and I am frightened. A kindly smile from him reassures me.

The bearer returns. He has wrapped the jacket in a clean towel. "Let the sahib take it back."

The Canadian mahatma laughs, and flings the jacket on the bearer's pile, and pats the bearer on the back. The bearer whispers to me, "If the sahib would like to stay here another night, I could make good arrangements for him." I ignore this.

The bearer makes an exasperating request. "Would the sahib please write a letter to the hotel manager to tell him that he has given the clothes to me of his own free will?"

The Canadian mahatma reluctantly sits down at the table and starts to write, in a shaky hand. Each piece has to be described and initialled. He reads aloud, "Sir: I give this bearer one silk dressing gown, also six silk shirts with French cuffs, two striped shirts and one white. One dinner jacket. Two suits . . ."

While the Canadian mahatma reads, the bearer retreats to the bathroom to return the towel. He does not come back until the list is completed. It is one-thirty. The bearer wants to carry the suitcase down, but the Canadian mahatma insists on carrying it himself.

By the time we get him to a taxi, he has only fifteen minutes to catch the plane. He throws his arms around us. "Boys, India is too much for me. I wish I could be Gandhiji. But I'm not a saint—just a filthy bastard."

I leave Dom and spend the rest of the day quietly at home.

Next morning, we are back at Khushwant's, but this time Khush-

want has his headdress on before we arrive. He seems to have
had a premonition about our restless wanderings. He's extremely
amusing. He says he has written his fifth book and titled it something like " I Shall Not Be a Nightingale;" he thinks it will sell
like " Lolita," which is, however, an immoral book, because since
reading it he has become overconscious of the friends of his
thirteen-year-old daughter, especially when he sees them around
the swimming pool. Khushwant says that from five to seven every
morning he has a Sikh priest come and visit him to take him
through the ancient Sikh scriptures.

We lunch with Narayana, and I think, from the way he holds
his silver, that he is an artist to his fingertips. Dom asks him if
he's heard of the pink girls. "The older sister worked in the
theatre, and sometimes her work was at night," Narayana tells
us. "To avoid incidents, she was given a driver and an escort.
In fact, it amounted to two drivers, who watched each other.
Door-to-door service, you know. Safe, secure, and very necessary
in a place like Delhi—indeed, throughout India. Well, one night
she worked until two-thirty, and as she was going from the theatre
to the car, there were loud screams in the corridor, and within
a matter of seconds a crowd had collected. She shouted accusa-
tions of intended rape. Many of the theatre people ran down
the corridor on a man-chase, but the assailant had too much of
a head start. A chance police car hunted him down. He claimed
to be innocent, but he admitted being in the building on a
friendly visit. He would not disclose the name of the friend, and
since the evidence was circumstantial, the girl was advised to
drop the case. But the mother wanted the man hanged, drawn,
and quartered, and the older of your little pinks claimed to have
met the fate of the heroine of 'A Passage to India.' The theatre
building became the Marabar caves. In the courtroom, it seemed
that the girl and the accused knew each other. One person had
seen them at the pictures together, and also there was a matter
of returning a book to the girl, which this gentleman had over-
looked. Naturally, the question arose: What book, borrowed
when? It was a farce." Narayana counsels us to beware of these
girls, and not to court them in the Western style. If we hold

hands with them, we should be prepared for a breach-of-promise suit.

In the evening, we wander into a rich neighborhood looking for a lady known to us as Miss Fulbright Fellowship. Khushwant has told us about her. "The quietest, gentlest soul walking in Delhi. Beauty and loveliness. But my name will be no recommendation for you." There had been a New Year's dance at the Golf Club, the smartest society represented. Khushwant had suggested the dance and made the arrangements. Guests were asked to bring bottles of whiskey, and since many of them were in the military or diplomatic service, they had access to tax-free liquor. Some brought as much as a case. Everyone heavily drank the New Year in—dancing, rollicking, rocking with delight. There were lots of left overs, and Khushwant was rewarded for his exertions with the unopened bottles. He was able to stock his cabinet with liquor for the following six months. This was one reason, among others, for his being the center of Delhi society.

By the time Khushwant caught sight of Miss Fulbright standing in a corner looking on at the party, he was high and merry. He thought she was moody. The hapless Khushwant rushed over to Miss Fulbright, gathered her in his arms, and began dancing.

"I can't dance! I can't dance!" protested Miss Fulbright.

Khushwant thought she was being shy, so he dragged her across the floor, back and around. When he stopped to catch his breath, he noticed her face tense with pain and realized she was lame. For Khushwant, the party was finished.

He lost Miss Fulbright as a friend, and she avoided him like a woman who has been roughly handled. But, whatever her judgment of Khushwant, he nursed only delicate thoughts about her. As he told us about the party, he blushed behind his big beard.

We cannot find Miss Fulbright. The street she lives on is strange. It has no order. The numbers of the houses leap from the tens to the hundreds, and it seems everyone has posted his lucky number on the door. The houses on the street are large and the numbers printed on them are large, too. When we finally reach her house, having had three wrong doors shut in our faces, we find a quietness and eloquence that we have never associated with foreigners in India.

The room is air-conditioned, but the machine, unlike those in less expensive houses, is far away; we can't hear the motor rumbling.

Miss Fulbright sits on a large sofa but somehow makes it small. She serves us small glasses of Dubonnet, which we sip. The conversation gets quieter and quieter, until all three of us are whispering, missing each other's remarks but somehow feeling happy in each other's company. She is excited about a project for using bullocks to generate electricity. "Wouldn't it be magnificent if the bullocks, which are idle during the winter, could be used to produce electricity half the year!"

"Is it successful? Have you tried it?" I ask.

"We have in a few villages," replies Miss Fulbright. "The bullocks keep in shape for the harvest and don't become lazy; villages get electricity without burning coal, and all the children turn out to watch the bullocks go round and round to light the lamps. I saw it some time ago and loved it. It was Indian and beautiful."

"But the real need for electricity is during harvest time," I say.

Dom says, "But surely bullocks are temperamental and will not move like dynamos."

And I ask, "How can you store electricity?"

Miss Fulbright says, "Oh, but this is the romance of the bullocks! This is the great thing for India. It uses the natural resources of the country. It also preserves the village community. Gandhiji would have liked that."

There is something about the way she speaks that makes the ridiculous convincing.

A friend of Miss Fulbright drops in. He is an aged professor of Sanskrit—simple and sedate, scholarly but not scholarly in an ordinary way. He recites Sanskrit poetry and makes us forget the time and the place. "The poetry I am reciting to you is something that may have been recited on the banks of the Ganges two thousand years ago—with exactly the same intonation, the same accent," he says. "The language has been preserved not on paper but in the memories of the people. Today you could go to Hardwar or Benares and hear Brahmans reciting Sanskrit poetry as though time had never moved."

I feel slightly uncomfortable when Miss Fulbright speaks English after his recitation. The English jars. But Miss Fulbright and the Sanskrit professor seem to share a quiet simplicity. They are less widely separated by language and generation than are most English and Indians. Somehow, Miss Fulbright seems to belong to India.

The bearer comes in and turns out the lights. Only candles are left burning. We can tell by Miss Fulbright's manner with the professor that she is in love with Sanskrit. I suspect another romance as well. We all end up reciting poetry to each other. When we leave, we leave behind us a beautiful evening.

Dom says in the taxi, "What a romance!"

"You mean the bullocks?" I ask.

"No, theirs."

"Dom, it couldn't be more impractical than the bullock experiment."

Dom says, "But it couldn't be lovelier, either," and we laugh.

We are alarmed at the prospect of tea with the pinks. Thank God for the mother. She settles down in the room.

There is also a third visitor, a general, who talks with the mother. The pink girls call him "General," and the general is angry and puzzled. "Why this big change?" he asks. "Until yesterday, you called me 'Uncle'. Why 'General' today?"

"General, General, General," says the younger pink defiantly. "General, General, General. I'm grown up now."

"You are a slip of a girl," says the general.

The younger pink puffs her mouth. The mother gestures, and the general is quiet. The older pink gets up and comes and practically sits on Dom's lap, and then says, "Excuse me."

We discover that the younger pink is still in a convent school, so we ask how old she is. She pouts. We drop the question.

The younger pink talks big. "I hate nuns," she says.

"Don't be silly," says the older pink.

"I go out every evening," the younger pink says, "and stay out until three o'clock."

The older pink says that this is wrong, and that she should recognize the importance of education.

The mother disappears, and the general, after bending down and giving both the girls a hug, goes away also.

The sisters begin talking about their friends.

"Have you heard of Gigi?" the younger pink says.

"Who's Gigi?" I ask.

"She's the most wonderful person in the world," she replies enthusiastically. "She's only fifteen, but she's writing a book, 'Nuns and Champagne,' and even Ruffles has kissed her."

"Who's Ruffles?" Dom asks.

"You know, *the* man-about-town," says the younger pink.

The older pink says he is stupid and silly.

The younger pink insists he is handsome and out of this world.

The older pink says, "Don't be silly."

The younger pink says to her sister, "Didn't he look handsome last night, at the party of the Moroccan diplomat? You must mention him in your column."

"Do you write?" I ask the older pink.

"Oh, just now and then, for a gossip magazine," the younger pink answers for her. "If you come to a party, she will include you in her list."

As the conversation progresses—or, rather, as the two sisters talk—the small, tidy sitting room becomes peopled with their shrill friends. They are the smart set, and all seem to be beautiful, gay, provocative—full of sex and charm. They all seem to love music, dancing, and our two pink friends.

Teatime expires. Anyway, it is hot and tedious, so we try to get away. But the girls stop us. "Stay for drinks," they say. And we do. Our spirits are considerably dampened when the servant dances in with a trayful of warm Coca-Colas. We drink the tepid drink. The conversation seems, finally, to have nothing but pauses. The girls won't let us leave them that evening without our fixing a time to return.

In the taxi, we swear to each other never again. "We don't belong in that smart set," I say, and Dom says, "But maybe we *need* pink girls. Or publicity agents. Or pink clouds. Or something." And we laugh.

Next day, we go to Delhi University. Dom and I have taken to speaking at colleges. Our performances are uneven, owing partly to our moodiness and partly to the variety of groups we have to read to and address. Everything in India is vague. You may get a telephone call in the morning with an invitation from a college, but until you arrive, there is no way for you to discover whether the audience will be composed of staff, students, or bystanders.

Once when I spoke at a women's college, the principal requested me to speak softly, because the hall had hidden microphones and perfect loudspeakers, and after I finished an hour-long lecture on American universities, I discovered that no one had been able to hear me, because the Delhi Electric Company had switched off the current, a usual expedient when there was a need to replace parts or to save electricity. The principal was proud of the girls because they were so well trained that although they couldn't hear a word, they pretended to hear and understand everything. "In England, the audience would have thrown tomatoes, or at least shouted," I said to the principal. She replied ironically, "There is no heckling in Indian colleges. We have only hunger strikes."

Dom and I have come to expect surprises from our speaking engagements.

When we arrive at Delhi University, we can't find the lecture hall. A dashing young man comes up to us and presents himself as a reporter. We introduce ourselves and together look for the hall. When we locate it, we discover that the meeting has started without us. The occasion is the anniversary of the English Union, or some such, and a wiry, nervous professor is lecturing on the virtues of the English language and English literature. His speech, which was to have introduced us, has become a paean to English: "Like everything in India, standards of teaching English are declining, even though English is five times a better language than Hindi, because English has five times the vocabulary of Hindi, yet no Indian can write decent prose in English or Hindi, because, in the first case, the language isn't refined and, in the second case, students have stopped studying the great masters of English prose—Chaucer, Shakespeare, Milton, Johnson, Molière, Goethe, Tolstoy." The professor appears confused, and he looks at his notes and asks the students, who are busily writing, to eliminate the name of Tolstoy. "As I was saying," he goes on, "the study of English has much to recommend itself and I do not mean only the study of words but the study of literature, for the learning of language is simply a means to an end, and we must never lose sight of the end, for end is everything. But that is not to say means are unimportant, for if that were so, there would be no end. I hope my meaning is clear." At the conclusion of his lecture, many heads in the audience are nodding, and there have been some desertions from the back row. The wiry, nervous professor finally looks up from his notes and sees us. "I want to now introduce you to literature which Mr. Moraes and Mr. Mehta have brought to us," he says, and then he breaks the back of yet another sentence. "On second thought," he continues, "I will let them be introduced by themselves as I do not wish to presume, and besides . . ." And so on and so forth.

I come alive with the poems of Dom. He reads them in a hurried way, as though he were reading words that he didn't understand—words that belonged to another language. Now and again, I detect a sort of irony in his voice and find him parroting his own poems. The audience, however, is attentively serious.

After Dom reads, I speak on fact and fancy, and tell of an English professor of mine who preferred fancies to facts, a novel to a history book, his gossip over an eleven-o'clock cup of coffee to the morning newspaper. "The world is a shoddy place, and no one can endure reality for long," he used to say. "We must all have escapes from the world and refresh ourselves at the burning fountain of literature. Man can transcend his infinitesimal experience only through imagination."

I talk about beauty, and recite verses and prose passages. Dom joins me in invoking beauty, and recites verses from poets past and present. It is great fun—sometimes a bit bizarre, because there are tiny laughs from the audience when we begin a quotation and can't finish it. Afterward, there is tea outside, and tea in India means a sort of supper—enormous quantities of food, hot, spiced, pickled. The undergraduates eat with their hands and suck their fingers clean. Every one of the students turns out to be an amateur palmist, and they fight for our hands. Two palmists win the scrimmage by virtue of superior age. They hold our hands in their palms and finger them as though they were kneading dough. The students sit around us in a circle on the grass. Dom's hand is read first. "You are poet to your fingertips," it is announced. "You will cross the seven seas seven times, you will have seven children, you will not always be happy. You will live to be seventy-seven."

Dom says he would rather have seven wives and the death of Dylan Thomas. That sort of death is more poetic. My hand is read and commented upon, but by the time my turn comes everyone is reading everyone else's hand.

The possessive pinks turn up to drag us away. Having smuggled themselves into the audience, they are generous with their compliments on our speeches; they treat us as if we were their protégés, and try to protect us from being mobbed.

They discourage students from being overfriendly with us and turn them from palmistry to horoscopes. At the end of tea, we are left with the prospect of spending another evening with the pinks. But Dom and I get lost in a vanishing act.

We lunch with Khushwant the next day. Lots and lots of Americans are there. A tall American girl, who is an adviser on manure, says Dom has the most beautiful face she has ever seen. Dom clears his throat two or three times, as he usually does when he's flattered, and doesn't know what to do with his hands. It's a strange lunch, for the Americans talk terribly loudly; we get the impression that many of the Americans in India are a mistake, but, of course, there's no way to test this. A queue of rats slides into a corner hole during the lunch. We don't feel hungry. We tease Khushwant about the rats, and he says they're a Delhi occurrence, and reminds us we are in India. We tell him about our pink girls, and then we try to be clever, and call their parlor the pink-light district. Khushwant says he knows them, and says they are innocent but pretty. During part of the lunch, Khushwant sits on the floor and drinks beer and grips the arm of a very fat American girl, and she says she will report him to the F.B.I. for having bad fingerprints. Khushwant laughs, but we don't think it's a frightfully good joke. We notice he doesn't let go of the arm, and his enormously attractive bearded face is turned up to the girl.

The ladies disappear into the bedroom, and Khushwant tells us an amusing story. During the war, he was forced by a group of men to go with them to a red-light district to keep them company. There he found six girls playing a very curious game with one G.I. They were kicking an old tin of boot polish from one side of the veranda to the other. The girls and the G.I. were breathless. Two girls, Khushwant, and the G.I. were left on the veranda after certain arrangements had been made among the others. And Khushwant, having only a "writer's interest" in going to the district, paced up and down nervously until the G.I. resumed his game and invited Khushwant to join, and there he was, kicking an old tin of boot polish around the veranda with two girls and a G.I., while the other men were with the girls inside. "Very, very tough game," Khushwant told us. "I was breathless, too, after fifteen minutes. After the game, one of the girls told me that they had tried everything to entice the G.I. He had been coming there for the last nine months, but he wanted nothing at all. He just wanted to play that game." Perhaps in India the pink cloud was a boot-polish tin. It was a thoroughly strange lunch.

Indeed, everything we did in India was strange. Or at least we thought it strange. Dom and I would entertain each other and whoever was with us by saying, for example, " Khushwant's lunch was very strange." It was a wonderful opening, giving us an opportunity to embellish and embroider little incidents. This was done not only to amuse our company with fantastically exaggerated accounts but somehow to find an escape from our own gloom.

We see a lot of the pinks. For one thing, there is nothing else to do, and, for another, while they are extremely boring to be with, in their absence they provide us with little rapturous ironies. One day, the girls haven't had any dinner, so the four of us go to the Volga looking for sandwiches. We're turned away, so we go to Gaylord's and get the girls some sandwiches and try to give them the slip. They will not accept excuses. All of us get into a taxi, and the girls help us look for a patch of grass, because Mother is expected home. We find a patch of grass, and while the girls unwrap the sandwiches we ask the taxi-driver to join us, and give him some sandwiches. The girls are hurt at our "democratic" hob-nobbing and talk in pig Latin about their disapproval. I have the embarrassing task of getting rid of the driver. I ask him to move the car, please. He, in turn, is hurt at the hint. We take a little walk, but the patch of grass is anything but exclusive. We stumble over some people. The air is cut with laughter and screams. The girls say they are homosexual screams. We are frightened by the unknown, and hurry back to the car and the protection of the driver. The girls lecture us about the social advantages of Delhi, about making our homes in India, about Ruffles, about Gigi, about the Moroccan diplomat, about the convenience of servants. Oh, the life is gay, social, and wonderful, but we feel depressed.

Dom says he can't write any poetry in India, so he must leave for England. I can't write, either. We begin to stay more and more in Dom's room, and come to love the rattle of ice in glasses, the whiff of strong drinks. We eat little and cover up the window-panes with shades. The pinks ring up eight times a day, but we pretend to be busy with our poems and novels.

We go to Narayana. He consoles us, and says perhaps we would enjoy seeing a man I choose to name Mr. Chatterji. He has been to England, though only for a few weeks, and yet manages to live and write in India. "He lives by the old Delhi wall," Narayana says. "One of the most successful Indian prose writers—disliked in India, loved in England."

"What's his address?" I ask.

"Don't know," Narayana says. "Just ask for the Bengali babu [gentleman]."

So we hail a taxi and ask to go to the Delhi wall—a slum area, like the East End in London or the lower East Side in New York, except that here the poverty is just plain horrid, naked on the streets. We ask a great many little children about the famous writer. They disclaim any knowledge of him. We describe him as a man of sixty, and a child pipes up, "I've never heard of anyone so old in this part." Laughter around us. We walk up and down narrow gullies, in and out of small, stablelike houses, but no Mr. Chatterji. "Oh, yes, I think I know him," somebody says. "Isn't he the one who goes to universities with a cloth bag, tall and handsome?" We pass on. Finally, we remember Narayana's advice about asking for the Bengali babu instead of Mr. Chatterji. We are directed to a rickety staircase—up one flight, up two flights, up three flights. We say the magic words "Bengali babu," and we are directed to go left. A shrivelled-up naked figure is sprawled out on a veranda. We take him for a servant of the great writer.

"Where is the sahib?" I ask.

The figure first squints, then looks at us, then points down the veranda. A second naked figure leads us down the veranda and shows us into the Bengali babu's drawing room. Two chairs, placed between two doors, catch the breeze in this room. The Bengali babu has no fan. We occupy the chairs, grow uneasy with waiting. Then the Bengali babu, the first naked figure we saw, now dressed, appears. He majestically sits down on the floor. "The man who showed you here was my son," he says. "My other son is studying in London."

We have met many eccentrics, but never one so eccentric as this. He lectures us about the inaccuracy of "A Passage to India" (Mr. Forster got the cast of the assize wrong). He calls us the children of darkness (without explanation). He says he knows more about English literature than anyone else in the world. "All my friends are foreigners," he says. "Indians don't like me, because I think. They want to crucify me. They call me a dog who wags his tail at the smell of London stew. I am so famous, and yet no Indian of my age has visited me. Khushwant and Narayana are exceptions. I get invited to two hundred diplomatic cocktail parties in a season, but I hate them, so I go to only seventy. I live here because it's the most Indian and most historic place in the world. I'm loved by the people of the old wall." He offers us coffee after an hour and a half of talk. I think we pity him more than like him. We invite him to lunch the next day and dinner the day after. We quote him eagerly. He is an Indian writer who can write in India; he is our hope in that darkened sky.

At lunch the next day, Mr. Chatterji shows an encyclopedic knowledge of English literature and geography and people. Strange, I think, to love England as he does and yet to have spent only a few weeks there. Strange, too, that he knows more about England than most Englishmen. It is sad that Mr. Chatterji should think of England as Christians think of God—without the mystical experience. Dom says, "England is Mr. Chatterji's pink cloud, but his England is not ours."

One morning, the darkness lifts and the face of the sun peers through the clouds. The writer Han Suyin is in town. A week in America, one television interview, and she cut short her visit by a month and came to Delhi. "Before you die," she says, "you must see Katmandu." Katmandu is, of course, the capital of Nepal. Feeling close to death, we decide to go to Nepal. Dom's father knows a general who lives there and in whose palace we can stay. The general is a Class A Rana. His family is second only to that of the King of Nepal, and up until a few years back, when there was a revolution, provided the country's Prime Ministers.

Khushwant, Narayana, and Han Suyin make Delhi for us, and we—Dom and I—make Delhi for each other. I remember the last conversation—tipsy and disorganized—with the pinks.

Dom : "The Dalai Lama awaits us."

Me : "Hum."

Dom : "We must go."

Me : "Yes, Dom."

The pinks : "Never, never, never, never, never."

Dom : "We must. The Dalai Lama awaits us."

Me : "After that, a plane to Katmandu."

The pinks : "We are coming with you."

Me : "We need them but we cannot afford them."

Dom : "Shall we go? What is the time?"

Me : "Late."

The pinks : "Not yet, please."

Me : "We must."

Dom : "We must. The tiny Dalai Lama awaits us, and then a tiny plane to Katmandu, then guests of tiny general living in tiny palace, tiny drinks, perhaps girlkins, tiny girlkins, tiny Nepalese girlkins. The Dalai Lama awaits us."

We get up. We are pushed back into our seats. We get up again, are bounced back into our seats. Tiny tears glisten in pink eyes. We discover that the younger pink is only fifteen. She goes into the bedroom, sulking, so we can't leave. A half hour of comforting.

Me : "We are late for the Dalai Lama."

The younger pink : "Dalai Lama, Dalai Lama, Dalai Lama! What is he to you? What are you to him?"

Dom : "A little appointment with him tomorrow."

The younger pink : "Tomorrow, tomorrow, tomorrow! But now it is today."

Me : "Need a good sleep."

The girls are angry. We promise to come back before Nepal. No wet pink goodbyes. Just departure. Another taxi, and we cut through the stifling air.

Next morning, we get into a tiny DC-3 and climb to six thousand feet. First stop, Agra—the Taj Mahal seen through haze from two thousand feet. Then Benares—rather pleasant. We get V.I.P. treatment. Invariably, people recognize Dom or me. We are seated and served coffee. Other passengers stand in queue. We wait at the airport for six hours. The stop is supposed to be only half an hour, but the weather is bad—monsoons. The clouds gurgle and thunder. The sky is all right for a Super-Constellation but bad for a DC-3. Finally, the airline people are discouraged. The flight is postponed, and toward evening Dom and I taxi to Clark's Hotel. The rooms are a present from the airline. Benares is the oldest city in the world, and when we pass the shops, they seem like museums. Very fat shopkeepers sit in small shops, selling antiquities, haggling. They surprise us, because they sit in front of their merchandise and hide it, like tourists obscuring museum treasures. The rooms in our hotel are like those of official resthouses—suites set behind vast verandas, which take the place of corridors. We feel frustrated, and are not in the mood for a tour. A bearer asks us whether we would like a gay night. We say no and order some whiskey. Dom takes his first drink in eight hours and finishes it in a long gulp. I begin to feel sick with waiting for the plane.

We pass the evening in the bar, talking with the pilot of the plane, who deplores the DC-3. He hates the monsoons. The pilot says, "God is really capricious, diabolical. If we have too much rain, we have floods, because of the mountains; if we have too little rain, we have famine. Rain or no rain, if we have clouds, we can't fly. If there are no clouds, we have sunstroke. The Hindu god is capricious. Why can't we have the spring of the Englishman and the autumn of the American? I have flown big Super-Constellations to London, and you have to see an English spring to believe it. All the kingdom of flowers smiles at you, and you feel in harmony. India is a rotten country. It has mountains, and the beauty of the mountains does delight the soul, but the mountains are the cause of the floods. It breaks my heart." The pilot spits in his beer glass.

We ask him if he would like some whiskey.

"No, thank you," he says.

"Don't you like whiskey?" Dom asks.

"I love it," the pilot says.

"Then why not have some?" I say.

"In India, I never touch whiskey," he says. "It's immoral. Too much poverty. It's like drinking blood."

Dom looks away. I pick up my glass and feel very sick at my stomach.

The pilot laughs a jolly laugh and says we are both very young. He thanks us kindly and says his good nights. Both of us go to bed soon afterward.

The next morning, we spring out of bed and run to the air office and then to the airport. The voice on the loudspeaker says, "There is a break in the clouds, and we shall be flying in half an hour." We are soon in the air, flying toward Katmandu. We sleep. Patna—last stop in India—is announced. We stroll out, then go back to the DC-3. As the plane bumps its way toward Katmandu, we reminisce about Han Suyin. She told us, "Katmandu is the most beautiful place in the world. It is a baptism of beauty. All the citizens of Katmandu are initiates into the cult of beauty, the cult of art, the cult of the gods." Dom's father called the general we are about to visit a "gay sea dog," and in our imagination we see him quilted in whiskey, women, and happiness. We bump and bounce into the valley, and we step majestically off the plane singing "Kat-man-du."

We experience a thrill as "Katmandu" is stamped on our passports. The general's chauffeur has met us at the airport. As we get into the car, we ask him what there is in Katmandu. What are the mystery and magic of Katmandu? What is its poetry? He says, "There is not much here to see. Most tourists come for the temples. It's a boring place." In English, Dom and I talk of people with drab imaginations. Majestically, superciliously, we drive toward the palace. It is like waking in a dream—sun on Katmandu, high walls of mountains, valley tucked in like a pocket of bliss, peaks all around us. No fog, no dust, no clouds— beautiful, balmy weather. We reach the general's palace, which seems to occupy almost half of Katmandu. We pass through enormous halls. On the walls all the generals of the world, all in Nepalese dress, seem to be queuing up for God knows what. Cathedral ceilings, velvet, antique furniture, ornaments, chandeliers, dimensionless—this is the palace.

F

We are shown to a drawing room and a sofa. We seem to be buried in satin cushions. We sink back and wait for the general. Instead, the queen of the house appears, elderly but preserved like a girl of eighteen. Only graying hair gives away her secret. She speaks to us in a strange tongue, and about strange, mysterious things. She seems to be apologizing for something. Finally, we are shown to our palace apartment. Five rooms. Each of our beds can hold a half-dozen people, and the mosquito net around it seems to enclose a secret world.

A son of the general is our host at tea. Eighteenth-century cutlery, delicate omelets, purées, and pastries. It is a perfect blend of East and West, of big and small. The whole palace is a brocaded simplicity. No paradoxes—only riddles. Nice little tiny lovely riddles. The son, who is about twenty and speaks English, tells us that in Nepal before the revolution of 1950 " general " was an inherited title; with Sandhurst irony and English wit, he tells us that most of the generals have sunken cheeks and broken backs, and that since Nepal is a peaceful country, most of the fighting is done in bed. We finish our tea and go back to our bedroom and look expectantly under the mosquito net and between the white sheets. There are no visible concubines. The servant unpacks our tiny bags and asks us if more are coming. He wants to lay out our dinner jackets. We have only hiking clothes—a couple of khaki shirts and some tatty trousers.

We are summoned to dinner. There are many other guests. The general welcomes us summarily, makes us feel that it is a great privilege even to be spoken to. We repeat our names many times, but he never gets them. There are stares from the other guests because of our clothes and shabby appearance. They seem to be insulted. The family seems huge. At least five sons are at the table, with their wives. I learn that all five of them lived in the palace and ran the politics of Nepal with their father before the revolution. I learn that the palace is equipped with its own bank, tailor, goldsmith, and watchmaker, and with a hundred servants. During coffee, I corner the general to ask him about the revolution.

"Wasn't there a revolution in Nepal a few years back?" I ask naïvely.

"It was the time when I lost my hundred and fifty concubines," he answers.

New definition of revolution, I think. "What happened during the revolution?"

"I lost my concubines."

Before the revolution, a Rana could ride his elephant, and all the women in Katmandu would crowd onto their balconies, eager for his attentions. If he waved at one, her fortune was made. She was taken into the palace. "No elephant rides now," he says. "The good old times are over. Now I have only seventy-eight maidservants."

I go off and whisper this fact to Dom, and we approach the general together. I begin, "You see, sir, most of our life has been spent abroad and we've never met a concubine. Do you think it would be possible to meet one now?"

Dom breaks in. "The B.B.C.," he says, in a Domlike gambit, "asked us to interview a few concubines in Nepal."

Three minutes' unnerving silence. Then the general announces militarily, "If you have any ideas about prowling around tonight, we have five Tibetan wolfhounds in the compounds." With that, he contemptuously gestures our dismissal.

Days in Katmandu are, for us, days of waking. We find strange things. The strangest of all is the naturalness of the surroundings and the people. Men and women work side by side in the fields. They sing and dance with their ids but are not embarrassed. The women are beautiful and healthy, and not, like Indian women, always pulling the folds of their saris to give them more drape. The sari is the winding sheet of sex in India, but not here. And here people are not made ugly by their poverty. For the first time since we came home, it really feels as though we were on a pink cloud.

A newspaper reporter, a friend of Dom's father, is our guide through Katmandu and Nepal. By his friends he is nicknamed Prince, because he knows every stone in Nepal. He has keys to all the secret doors that open into mysterious places. He hires us a jeep, and our first visit is to a nearby village to see a great lama, an émigré Buddhist priest from Tibet. We have an audience with him. He speaks twenty-four languages, and his first question to our guide is: What would we like on the language menu? After choosing English, we settle down in chairs made of tree bark to listen to the Buddhist priest. He talks like the editor of a posh magazine. He is suave, smooth, and grand. He lectures us about suffering and sacrifice, about having infinite love, about fleshly snares, about the necessity of meditation and pursuit after truth, about faith in the ancient wisdom. His day consists of six hours of meditation, three hours of prayers, four hours of instruction to his disciples. He counsels us to follow his path. It is very strange, because after Dom, in one of his gambits, has told him about our "artistic pursuits" and said that we were thinking of settling down in Nepal as permanent residents, he is no longer the great lama, the ascetic Buddhist. He opens his cupboard and offers us some homemade gin. "They don't have better gin in England," he says. We drink it avidly, from imported glasses. His three wives serve us Chinese tea, which has a kind of mixed flavor of jasmine and gin. Then enormous plates of food are brought, after which the great lama goes for a nap and we are entertained by the many children of the household. Disciples of all ages and both sexes drift in and out. They seem to adore the great lama, for they come bearing sweets and fresh vegetables— potatoes with clinging mud, and tomatoes red and the size of apples.

We walk to the center of the village in the afternoon. Prince can't go with us. He says he must get back to Katmandu, because there is a Communist procession, the first such in Nepal to protest against Dalda Ghi, a government-sponsored margarine that, according to the Indian Communist Party, gives people coronary thrombosis. There is no evidence for this, but since the government now allows the sale of Dalda Ghi it is necessary that "people should know the truth."

All the adults are in the fields, except for a few old people draped over doorsills, sunning themselves. The village seems to be inhabited by children alone. They follow us in a procession of a hundred into the outskirts, on our way to the temple, and laugh at our feeble attempts to go through thickets and along one-man trails. Dom says we must get horses tomorrow, because they would be more sure-footed.

In the evening, there is a reception for Dom and me at the house of a poet. All the littérateurs of this tiny country meet us and treat us like celebrities. We are a bit embarrassed and uncomfortable, and pray that our Soho friends will not see an account of our reception in print. The beauty, the magic of Katmandu, the mystery of concubines and palatial halls, the delicate, natural people all make us want to be natural, too, and it is difficult to be natural when being honored. Men twice our age sit with straight posture and read Nepalese poems in English and then wait for our judgment. But we have no offerings for the Nepalese gods. A terrible feeling, because they ask not for sacrifices of lambs but for little tiny comments. We pity them and feel guilty and don't know what to say. Partly it is the reading; the tone is flat, and the words are lisped and whistled. Partly it is the translation, for English is very much a second language to the translators. Partly, it is the nature of the poetry—Wordsworthian, just a little too mushy, a little too much of cows thinking pathetic fallacies.

We ask the rest of the poets to read their poems in Nepalese first, and somehow even the whistled words sound beautiful and are music to the ears—rhythm, intensity, power. And then the tedious English noise. Senses are confused. Perhaps some of them feel it, too, for a poet starts to read three poems and stops with one. It takes a little gentle persuasion to get him to read on.

The man who is capable of judgment—a greater celebrity than either of us, the poet laureate of Nepal, L. P. Devkota, nicknamed Mount Everest—is not present. His absence is felt. Many people tell us about him: "He has done more for Nepal than any other man in history." "He is the greatest genius we can claim." "He is the jewel of our country." "He has made most of us famous." "He has no time for small talk." "No man thinks more than he does." "His conversation is oracular. It is never vacuous but always breathes emotion, passion, and wit."

We keep our eyes fixed on the door, thinking that the poet will walk in at any time with crown and sceptre and make magic.

"When will he come?" I ask.

"Oh, didn't you know? He is dying. He's at Pashupatinath."

"What is that?" I ask.

"The greatest temple in the world."

There's a mysterious custom in Nepal. Men must die at the side of a river. The gods are kind, for four large rivers run through Nepal so that there is no village from which a dying man cannot be carried to his unction by the water. Pashupatinath is on the bank of one river. "Devkota allows his relatives to carry him to the river, but laughs at the custom. Three times they have taken him, but he won't die, and so they return him to the hospital."

"How long did he stay?" Dom asks.

"Two, three days each time."

The picture is disturbing. Several dying men laid side by side on stretchers, waiting, as it were, in a queue to be received by the water. And the poets alone have the license to laugh.

After their recitation, the poets force me to make a formal speech introducing Dom. I rise to the occasion; I mean, I realize that there is no point in telling any private facts about Dom, for although they would suit the atmosphere of Soho or Chelsea, which Dom once likened to a warm animal, they are out of place in this fairyland of Katmandu, with its magical people and magical language. He was born, I announce, in 1938; wrote tiny poems from the age of five; wrote a book on cricket at twelve; was admitted to Jesus College, Oxford, at eighteen; at nineteen wrote a tiny book that received a literary prize in England; and Dom is a legend. Dom thereupon says nice things about me and my writings, and, in his beautiful reading voice, he reads a poem of his called "A Letter to Dorothy." It is auto-biographical—a sort of letter to love. Childhood in Bombay, where the sun rules the dung-smeared plains, chauffeurs drowse on hot verandas; exile, family trouble; rain in England, three winters of lust and playing drunken king, when poems grow like maggots in his head; and then the great good news—spring and love, the hawk and serpent touched. He reads it beautifully, more beautifully than anything he has read in India. In his Indian readings he was resentful, because he was not sure whether the people understood English poetry. "A Letter to Dorothy" is specially appropriate here—prosy, straightforward, images sensuous, common thought. It is effective because of the personal revelation it contains. It makes him the center of attention. The assembled talent regretfully plead the deficiencies of their language, the inability to translate their thoughts and feelings, manifold and towering in Nepalese. "To be a poet in Nepalese is to die of frustration," one of them says. They wish they had been born in England. Our pity changes into sympathy, and the tenseness, the feeling of "I and thou," disappears. We are one. Dom reads a short poem about a Jesuit friend reading the river like a book of ancient wisdom, and then there is a libation, a praying for good fortune for one another, and we jeep across to the palace, silent and happy. The gods are good in Nepal. They live in Katmandu and ignore the people down south, who live in the shadow of the British raj, and with sunstroke, monsoons, and flood. Katmandu's sky is clear, all the stars are visible, and a good destiny is marked out.

Back at the palace, we have a tiny conversation with the servant given to us by the general. We are inquisitive and a bit tipsy from wine, stars, and delight. Dom asks him, "What do the seventy-eight maidens do?"

Embarrassment on the other side, but not so much as one expects. Understanding of our foreignness, I think. "They give pleasure in bed, and they bring silver pots for the Ranas," the servant says. The servant of enlightenment disappears in that natural, sweet way that we have come to regard as characteristically Nepalese.

We descend into our large beds, but the servant has chased away our sleep, and, what's more, he returns and says that if we had come before the revolution we would have been locked in with visitors sent as part of the hospitality. I regard this as another definition of revolution. Outside, the telephone wires sing duets with the crickets. We say good night to each other, and then I say a long prayer to the Nepalese gods. I compliment them on being so approachable, on giving men a chance to play, walk, and talk with them, on not living so far away, behind darkening clouds, as the gods do in other countries. I compliment them also, without feeling inferior to them, on their pinkness, on having only pink clouds for their dress, on not winding sex in a sari, on a hundred other things, and by and by I float into a wonderful long sleep, and when I wake, at noon, the soft sun lights the soft beauty of Katmandu.

It is two hours before the plane to Calcutta—back to the multitudes, back to the harsh sun, back to the dung-smeared earth. Our reporter guide, Prince, comes up to us. "You cannot go back to India until you've met Devkota," he says.

We tremble. Neither one of us has been to a deathbed. We are terrified. "No, thank you," I say. "We must go and pack."

"Don't tell me," Prince says chidingly, intimidatingly, "that you can't spare one half hour for a dying poet. He will be so flattered."

A poet laureate flattered by our visit?

Prince forces us into the jeep, and we are rattled toward the temple of death a few miles away.

What does one do? What does one say? We haven't spoken a word to each other. Prince is sitting in the front seat and we are in the back. And Dom says to me, or to himself, "You are being melodramatic." I have said nothing and I say nothing, but hold on to the steel frame of the jeep.

We are there at the river. From a distance it looks clear. It looks something like the Ganges, but the half-naked old women who are washing their clothes seem somehow prettier. There are the death chants, the mourning noises, the gnawing smell. We clamber up broken staircases, but our hearts are going down. We feel that the altitude is dropping, somehow, and the heart is feeling the pull of gravity too much. We are in the room. It is the season of flies. I long to breathe spring air. Around me are close to twenty relatives; the room is crowded and hot. A woman is fanning a figure wrapped in white sheets. The figure hardly has face or features, but his shrivelled hands feebly wave to us. Prince takes his position by the feet of the man. I don't know what to do. You see, the poet is lying on the floor, on a kind of mattress that covers the whole floor. There is no time to take off shoes. We have to sit quickly, relieve the tension of the room.

Through a window the stretchers of at least ten dying men are visible outside by the river. We can't keep our attention fixed on him, the poet. Soft groans. A very old man is breaking some ice and popping it into the poet's mouth. The woman goes on fanning. Prince introduces us in Nepalese. We can hear our names as Prince introduces us repeatedly. The poet gives us his hand. It's warm with life, and I feel calmed and soothed. He takes another piece of ice, and then the groans stop. He starts his speech slowly, as though he were drugged by death, but it is comforting to hear his voice. He thanks Prince for bringing these "two geniuses" from India. He seems to regard India as Dom and I regard England. He begins, "Christians are much better than we Hindus with death. They play music and they tell you about the heavenly angels sent for you, and the priest gives his unction with soft words and tells you if you really repent you will be taken up to Heaven. But Pashupati [the god of the animals] gives us Hindus no peace. He has robbed me of rest, he is cracking my soul. Pashupati will not give me any peace." Some more groans, then a smile of death plays on his face, ever so gently. "I don't know whether I believe in any of it. I would be better off in the hospital than here by the waters." A long pause. "I weighed two hundred pounds. Now I weigh ninety. You are seeing simply the skeleton of a man. Pashupati is cracking my soul and is burning me with cancer. No hell or fire could be worse than this. Give me your blessings, give your blessings to a dying man."

I stroke his hand and feel the Judgment Day.

He takes some more ice. "This is good," he says. "It quenches the fire. I wonder if there will be ice on the other side of the water. No torture could be worse than this cancer." His featureless face becomes more expressive, and I think perhaps he has said everything he has to say to all the relatives, and in this last moment of struggle he needs strangers.

Of Devkota's hundred written works only a few have been published. But he has tried to help the younger Nepalese poets. He asks what we think of his English translations and the anthology of Nepalese poetry that he edited, and is genuinely interested in our opinion. He says to Dom, "Will you recite some of your lines? I may not be able to understand now, but perhaps you could give me the gist of it."

First it is "A Letter to Dorothy," then "Mountains and Angels," then "Love and Courage."

"I wish I had command over English like that," Devkota says. "Someone like you should learn Nepalese and translate us for the world. We have the feelings but not the language."

Then some words of gentle advice. He counsels us to make India great, to work, like Mr. Nehru, in spite of suffering and frustration. "Do your duty and do not look for recognition or rewards," he says. "This has been my creed, and it has helped me to live and make my contribution to Nepal."

Soft groans, softer and softer groans. There is a feeling of utter helplessness all around us, except for the woman fanning and the uncle cracking ice. "It is a matter of minutes now, and I shall be out on one of those stretchers and this will be the last time," he says. We grow aware of our clumsiness. I am grateful that Dom can recite poems. Prince is looking out the window. Then he turns around and beckons to us to follow him. The poet is unconscious, so there are no words of parting to be said.

We go down the stairs awkwardly, feeling our way out of Pashupatinath. We jeep to the palace. Then there is a debate between Dom and me—the first words spoken since Pashupatinath—about what to give the servant. He is probably used to dinner jackets or gold chains, but we hand him our tiny rupee notes—as many as we can find in our coat pockets. Out of the twists and turns of the halls; a last, sweeping look over the chandeliers, the dimensionless; the servant brings the bags, and the general comes down to bid us a brief goodbye.

As our DC-3 takes off, the sky is threatening, and we are not sure about the ability of the plane to cut through the dense clouds. Soon the valley shrinks to the size of a postage stamp. The nose of the plane is directed toward Calcutta. Dom asks me repeatedly whether the poems he recited to Devkota were appropriate, and we end up talking about our unhappiness at being taken for more than we were, and about how our drinking friends in Soho would never forgive us for blessing the dying poet. But we console ourselves. The poet himself will forgive us. It is time to sleep.

We wake in Calcutta. Darkness of the deep night around us— steaming heat and torpor and Calcutta feigning to be London. Stucco is English, but many-colored stucco is Indian. The sun has bleached out the color. Some taxis have two drivers, because it is not safe for anyone, even a taxi-driver, to go it alone in Calcutta. We look for second-class hotels, but we don't like their façades, and end up at the Grand, which is the most expensive. Money-changers everywhere; thousands of doorways to staircases; a hotel for transients, people on the move. The predatory bearers swarm, hungry for baksheesh, even though the hotel is plastered with "No Tipping" signs. In our rooms, we order drinks, and two bearers carry them in, with an immense amount of ice and a number of ice towels. Dom thumbs through a telephone directory looking for people to call; we can think of no one. I pick up the telephone and put it down and have another drink. The heat in Calcutta is like the heat of a brick wall. We drink some more, and then we remember that prohibition is not enforced in Calcutta, so we go out into the streets. We hop into a taxi and say drive on. People are dying on the streets; human corpses are strewn like flies; women are giving birth to stillborn babies. Dom says that we will have to learn to live with the face of death in Calcutta. It is ten, and we are still driving around on a sightseeing tour of Calcutta with our eyes shut. Then we finally gain courage and ask one of the drivers to recommend a "bar with life," and he drives us through slums and slums—little dark doorways and unpainted wooden gates. He tells us a grisly story about people being knifed in bars, and asks if we wouldn't like to go back to the Grand. Some of the bars we pass are closed, and the driver says it is too late for a bar with life. But we persist, and have him wait outside a dingy entrance. The bar has nothing in common with English ones. No nucleus of sober people—just drunk after drunk, or tables with solitary girls of every possible nationality and color. We pass between tables lined up by the hundred, and look for a bar with a rail and stools. The rooms are dark and the music is loud, and the waitress thinks we are looking for trouble and pops us down at a table and insists on three drinks each and says we won't be alone too long.

We leave the drinks and money on the table and retreat into our taxi. I want to go to a bar with a rail and stools. The driver thinks we are looking for trouble, and says he has a family of seven waiting for him and all the nice girls are gone from the streets and bars and there is no point in wandering. We have nowhere to go, so he shifts us into another taxi, with a driver who drives fast and recklessly. This one says lots of bars are open, and takes us to a zoo, where monkeys, gorillas, and gibbons are being served drinks, and lots of sheep, pretending to be women, are crying in the corners, but we have found the bar with the rail and stools. We are served imported brandy, but it tastes like methylated spirits. We drink a quantity of it. Dom asks me whether I would like to go to Shillong, in Assam, and spend some weeks there studying the Nagas, the last of the head-hunters—or would I rather go to Sikkim, which is like Nepal? We think of many, many ways of getting out of Calcutta. But we take to the methylated spirits like ducks to water, and before long we are looking around the bar for little Siamese girls or tiny Persian women who would just talk to us about our troubles and depression. The barman asks us if we would like to meet some people. "First-class Anglo-Indian girls," he says. "Or European. But if you don't mind some dirty color, I have some beautiful children who will give you a good time." We go out into the street, and back to our taxi.

A series of disastrous accidents. First, as we taxi through one of those darkened streets, a blowout, and we lose our trustworthy taxi-driver. From the street, we enter a small, square room where there is an ugly dancer, riddled with all the diseases under the sun, who dances to all the scratchy records, and changes the needle more than she shuffles her feet. She pleads an empty stomach. A quilted floor, with round pillows for back rests. The harmonium players and the breathless tabla players and the girl of sixteen who dances and pulls at her hair and makes lascivious gestures and sings, "Nightingale is knocking at your door. Why don't you say come in?" She sings until one can almost see her lungs hanging out between her lips. We want to go home. Pimps are alerted from door to door, and there is no way out of the streets. A new, less dependable pair of taxi-drivers are cleaning out our pockets. They insistently and slowly take us from door to door, and rows of girls come up to the side of the car, and we take refuge by saying, "No, no." The girls walk away insulted and angry. Some of them say, "You are inhuman and callous." We give them some money. We spot another taxi standing, and, after paying our drivers, jump out of our car into it. "The Grand—quickly, the Grand!" One of the drivers starts the car—a long, rumbling sound in the engine, then an even hum. We sigh with relief. Before the taxi moves an inch, a man jumps halfway through the front window beside the un-occupied taxi-driver. He straddles the door—an ugly, bony face peering at us with bloodshot eyes, a hand holding a ridiculous little penknife. The unoccupied taxi-driver and the man on the window fight. The other driver accelerates the car and rushes through the street like a madman. The front door, which the man is straddling, opens and sags with the burden, but he clings on. He wraps his hands around the back door, and both Dom and I get down on the floor. Then there is the most terrifying scream, which rings through the streets like a death gong. The taxi man who is not driving has the figure by his testicles, and before Dom and I can get any words out of our throats the figure is dropped on the street and left. "Stop! Stop!" we shout at the driver. "You've murdered him." But the car is still rushing through the streets. The driver is trying to close the front door. He bangs the door violently and repeatedly.

"The bloody man was a robber. He got what he deserved." Then we are beneath the large, blinking neon sign : "THE GRAND." The driver gives us one big push out of the taxi. Before we recover, the car disappears into the alley and the dark night.

Upstairs, we collapse in our chairs. Our wallets have been pinched by the taxi-driver. We watch the dawn creep in through the window, and I feel heavy, as though I were carrying some dead weight.

Dom and I don't meet the next day until noon; we just stay in bed. And then Dom comes over and we sit at the table and ring for the bearer. Dom says he doesn't want anything to drink; coffee will do. The bearer doesn't understand our new interest in coffee. We drink coffee until two-thirty, and Dom paces nervously, sometimes stopping at the window. But there's nothing to see. It looks out on the courtyard and on other windows. Some of them still have their shades down. Dom starts reciting poetry. He has an excellent memory—a kind of poet's memory. He's not good at analysing things or explaining them, but he's excellent at remembering poems and conversations. By three-thirty, we are our usual selves, because we have cheered each other with odd poems.

I wonder if there are any people like Narayana or Khushwant here, and Dom starts thumbing through the telephone directory. Bengal is the house of literature, and this time a thousand names come to mind. We ring up the house of the poet Sudhindra Datta, but he's in America. The painter Jamini Roy doesn't have a telephone. We put down the telephone, and Dom drinks his twentieth glass of water. We slump on the comfortable divans and reminisce about our host in Nepal. Somehow we run through our stock of amusing stories quickly, and we both begin to pace nervously.

Dom rings for the bearer, and I notice that he has gone off water. After a couple of drinks, I switch to tomato juice. We call the poet Buddhadeva Bose on the telephone, and reach him. We stop feeling friendless. Bose would love to come for drinks, and he wishes to bring his cousin and an American poet. At seven o'clock, we try to find our way downstairs but get lost in the halls. We pass through an enormous room—hundreds and hundreds of people. A very loud, smoky cabaret. Someone is singing through a hundred loudspeakers, and the loudspeakers seem to be vying with one another. We rush through the maze, feeling tired and unhappy, and down flights and flights of stairs. We go into the Scheherazade Bar and wait and wonder about Bose's appearance. I long for a breath of fresh air, but Dom says he can't face the people outside. "Besides, there's no fresh air there," he says. "We are in a desert."

Bose arrives with his cousin and the American poet. Bose is a little man, Napoleonic, with a nervous face, animated eyes. He doesn't look like a poet, but he recognizes Dom as one. We go out on the veranda, because Bose is suffocated in the bar. We drink to each other's good health and then take a large taxi to Bose's house. People cling to the car, thrusting their emaciated hands in through the windows. The cousin puts up the windows. The American poet doesn't say very much. Gentle, handsome face, bangs of hair turning gray. The cousin says there are ten people in India who know how to write English; he and his cousin are two of the ten.

Bose is terribly nice, and upstairs in his little house he shows us his writings—scores of books in Bengali. He is the modern Tagore, but he lacks a translator. The American poet says that if he can find money he will spend a year in Bengal learning Bengali and then translate Bose for the world. The cousin says, "I have had precisely the same thing in mind, but then, on second thought, I think I ought to get on with my own creative work." The cousin reminds us about the big bills at the Grand and tells us we should come and live with him and talk art. We have dinner—fish with bones, which we enjoy separating. And after the fish we have liqueurs and talk of Tagore and Bengali literature, culture, and Communism.

But somehow Calcutta doesn't seem to be Delhi. It lacks the magic of our meetings with Khushwant, Narayana, Mr. Chatterji. And the strange thing is I am sure I like Bose just as much as the others, But things have changed. During the conversation, I have long lapses when I stop thinking, when I am there but not really there. My Oxford cigarette is burning very low, and if I am not careful the fag end will scorch my lips. There don't seem to be very many draws left.

When we leave, Bose comes along, and we visit Jamini Roy, but the paintings and the painter and some disciples at his studio —none of them make any impression upon me. I think I've never met a man like Jamini Roy—kind and compassionate, a grandfather to the human race. But somehow I can't make any effort to reach him, and continually find myself turning away toward a blank spot on the wall. Bose says he will arrange a party for us and gather some men of letters. But I cannot bring myself to be excited.

We are back in the Grand. Dom says that after Bose's party he will leave Calcutta and go to Sikkim, then to Bombay and back to England. He asks me whether I'd like to come to Sikkim, too. "It will be like Nepal," he says. "A pocket of private and delicious happiness." But I must go to Delhi. "I don't think I'll stay on for the party," I say. "I need a complete change. I think I will leave tomorrow."

Next day, I say goodbye to Dom. Dom insists that he must come to the airport, because he doesn't know when we will see each other again. Another leave-taking, and then a Viscount. I pinch myself, as I often do when I am going through a mad waking dream; then I nervously study my hands for the impressions of my nails, and I am relieved to find them there. The Viscount, once it is off the ground and the whistling sound has stopped, sounds like thunder—monsoon thunder, which makes protracted gurgling sounds before a blast—and I don't feel very well. I feel as if I were speeding away—far, far away from Oxford. It seems that my pilgrimage up north is over. The collecting of exhibits is over. The bummy period has ended. I feel old.

4

BETWEEN THE TWO WORLDS

Delhi begins to cool. It is too early for the mountain winds, and, as always, winter is slow in coming. But we stop sleeping on the veranda, stop being wakened by crows at dawn. The mosquito nets are put away, because winter is coming, and the doors and windows shut against what flies and mosquitoes remain. The summer of our discontent is ending. In Delhi, it never gets very cold. Although at night everyone must sleep under blankets, in the day time the edge of the winter is broken by the soft sun.

At home, Mother engages a tailor, who comes about nine-thirty every morning and stays for seven or eight hours to make winter clothes for the family. He does his own measuring, cutting, and sewing, and is as good with English suits as he is with shirts and casual wear. The tailor sits on our veranda. He has been working for us for many years. In the days before his family and ours fled from Pakistan, he made my rompers and knee pants, and when I graduated to wearing long pants, he put them on me and slapped my behind three or four times to remind me of my manhood. "But, Ved Sahib," he added quickly, "you will always be a boy to me."

Our tailor is Indian in his ways. He is not methodical. He is slow, spontaneously jocular, and able to entertain us for weeks with the saga of his family. He seems to remember every little thing that has ever happened to his grandparents, his aunts and uncles, his nieces and nephews. He will tell the sahib all the family troubles—how he is forced to work so many hours, and how difficult it is to pay for his children's education. And would it be possible to get his son a job in a government office, and couldn't you speak to So-and-So about his daughter, who would like to serve in a good house and would be a very faithful servant? When he has the ear of a sahib, he grumbles, and for a piece of good work he expects to be rewarded with favors. We feel personally involved with him.

Unlike many other Indian tailors, our tailor is never on the lookout for new employers. All his customers seem to be of twenty years' standing. He always complains about the many demands made on him. Recently, he was persuaded by a patron of nearly half a century to take on a new job. This, the latest exasperating demand, he was unable to refuse. "After all, Prasadji, the President of India, is in need," the tailor said. "At first, I didn't think I could take on his work, too. It is not just a matter of doing a job for Prasadji. He has dozens of children and grandchildren. Well, taking on his house is like taking on a whole new world of customers, and I'm very old and overworked."

Our tailor, though unassuming in appearance, claims he can change a man by changing the style of his clothes. He can transform babu into sahib, sahib into officer. Saint, beggar, bapu (father)—nothing is beyond him. His confidence is unnerving, and the only thing that makes him real is his endless family saga. He is very anxious to make me a new suit, using my English clothes as a model. He longs for a chance to rival English tailors, but many of his customers are politicians and have stopped wearing English clothes. "Sahib, may I make you a suit?" he asks.

I seldom go out now, and one light woollen suit is enough. "No, thank you," I reply. "I don't need a new suit." Instead, I ask him to make me another pair of pajamas and a *kurta*—a long, collarless shirt that hangs around the body like a sack. Loose pajamas and *kurta* are now my comfortable, homely dress. The tailor is disappointed, because this simple Indian dress demands no craftsmanship, no special tailoring. Because I am now staying at home more and more, I hardly ever wear a suit, though whenever I go out I put on my English suit, because I have grown used to it and it still seems dignified. Even my tailor can't redo a man overnight. But I am no longer aware of hand-sewn collars, three front buttons, and two slits in the back of the coat. I couldn't care less about gentlemanly elegance.

The tailor is the last of our old servants; the two house servants are new. I feel a bond with him, because he has watched me through my changing years. I can hear the slap of my bare feet when as a child I ran races with forbidden street children, the old servants watching and scolding and flattering, the tailor among them, shouting "Watch out for your clothes!" and, in the same breath, "Don't stop! Get on with you!" They smiled whether I won or lost. Sometimes my parents reproved me for being too close to the servants, but when they were out at offices and shops, at parties and clubs, the servants remained home as companions and storytellers. The children next door moved away when their father was transferred to another district, but the servants grew up with me; they never changed.

The tailor sits on the veranda of our new house, turning the wheel of his sewing machine. I recline in a wicker chair on the small lawn in front of the veranda. I am thirsty. I get up and bring two glasses of water, one for the tailor and one for me.

"Sahib, you should have asked me to get you some water," the tailor says. "Don't you like me anymore?"

"What is the difference?" I ask. I sit back in my chair and contemplate him. He is lean and frail, with a chest clamped between round shoulders, a bald head, and a yellowed beard, rich with the color of age. He stops turning the wheel, leaves his stool on the veranda, and comes and sits on the ground at my feet.

"Take this chair, take this chair," I say, nervously standing up.

He puts his gaunt hands on my knees, and I drop back into the chair. "Sahib, don't you like me anymore?" he says. "It's little things about you that trouble me. You won't let me cut you a suit like your English one, because you don't trust me. You don't let me get you a glass of water, because you don't like me. What has England done to you?" He won't remove his hands from my knees, and he stubbornly keeps his position on the ground.

"Look, tailor, I don't want an English suit because I am comfortable in pajamas and *kurta*," I say.

"Sahib, I don't understand the world. Why have people stopped wearing suits? Why have all the Indian gentlemen started wearing ugly black coats with buttoned-up collars? Why does everyone want to look like his poor tailor? What is going to happen to my profession? When I saw you in the beautiful English suit, my heart went out to you. The deputy high commissioner who used to live next door to you in the old days—do you remember him? He had a suit just like yours. Won't you let me cut you another? Never mind the rest of my customers. I'll work for you, Sahib, day and night, and it will be the best suit made in Delhi this year."

"But, tailor, you don't understand," I say. "A new English suit is the last thing I need. And about the water—I can get it as well as you can."

"Ved Sahib, your old servant and friend that I am, I would rather have you kick me than bring me a glass of water."

I try to explain to the tailor that he and I should be able to get each other water without his being hurt. But he sits at my feet holding my knees and refuses to accept my explanation. He feels offended. I stand up and nervously motion to him to sit down in the chair. He seems even more hurt, and shakes his beard. "What has England done to you?" he says. "I don't understand. I could never sit in that chair, and you know it. I have never sat in a chair, and I don't want to." As in the old days, the understanding really comes from him. I sit down. "Maybe I'm just old," he says. "Maybe I'm just ancient. Many of these young servants would like nothing better than a soft chair; they would let this grass grow under their feet until they were buried in it. They wouldn't lift a hand to cut it. By their rebellion they dig their own graves, and, Sahib, you aren't helping them learn their station by offering them chairs."

"Tailor, there is no station," I say. "Everyone must make his own station."

"No, Sahib," he says. "We are born into our station." He points to his scarred forehead. "My station is written here."

Then he points to my forehead. "Your station is written there. It is all in the books of karma and dharma. My karma says I must be a tailor and my dharma says I must do my duty by my Sahib."

"Tailor, these are old ideas."

"I am an old man," he says, and he runs a finger through his yellowed beard. "But, Sahib, I am wise. You can no more change my station than I can change yours. You will marry in your caste, and I will marry my son to a girl in our own caste. You will send your children to England to be educated, and I will teach my grandsons to be good tailors."

No, there can never be intermarriages between castes, he says, because his son will never have the education to marry above his station. No one can ever be swept away by love when marriages are arranged, and marriages must be arranged, because the parents' security and comfort in old age depend completely on their children. The older and the younger generations must be kept together. And so life must be perpetuated, so it must go on. No one can change the system, because the system is life. Then the tailor acknowledges that perhaps the times are changing. Someday all will be educated, but not yet.

Though he loves Englishmen, and therefore England, he chides me for my English ways. "Sahib," he says, "you're Indian, and not English." Then he turns to his machine and spins the wheel, circle upon circle, stopping now and again to give me counsel. He recommends a visit to Hardwar, where for untold centuries Indians have washed away their sins and deposited the ashes of their dead. At Hardwar is the source of the Ganges, in folklore the first spring of water in the Indian plains. It was the first water from the mountain, the great gift of God.

The suggestion strikes me as bizarre. My English self recoils from the centuries of superstition behind his words. But somehow I feel compelled to visit Hardwar.

A few days later, I travel to Hardwar. The tailor has admonished me not to wear my new pajamas and *kurta* until I am washed in the Ganges, and though I take his admonition lightly, I have brought them with me in a small case. Just to please the fancy of an old man—that is what I say to myself.

I want to ride in a third-class compartment to travel through India as Gandhi did, but my family won't permit it; there is danger of disease. This is my first train ride in India since my return. I like my carriage well enough—open windows, the seat covered with soot, the ineffective fan buzzing, and the blackening wind rushing in until it is impossible to make any conversation. I don't care about the people in my first-class compartment, because they are in English dress, with money in their pockets.

In the train, I become aware of country scenes: Gandhi's India—peasants with loincloths around their bodies, working on the land, tending the animals. Shifting images pass before me: Victorian, Civil Service, English India, with tremulous whispers about sex and with smoking-room banter. Political India, with circus legislatures. Intellectual India, with a Sanskrit text. Indias are endless.

People come to Hardwar with jars containing the ashes of their dead, or they come to wash away their sins, to be reinvigorated, to be cured of faults and diseases. The station at Hardwar is their hotel. Men, women, children eat and sleep there. The cows mill through the streets as if they owned them. Motorcar drivers hoot their horns impatiently. Religious music, played by beggar saints, drones continuously. At the river, I take my shoes off and walk along the bank until I find an uncrowded place. The Ganges, like the slow-moving Isis at Oxford, smells rank. A woman at my left drops some ashes in the river while reciting a Sanskrit prayer. I hold my breath, take a quick dip in the river, and rub myself vigorously with a towel. Then I put on my tailor's clothes. Around me, men and women stand half naked and say their prayers.

The genealogists—the Pandas—of India's hundreds of districts dwell at Hardwar. I walk up and down the bank looking for the Panda of my own village—my Panda, the Panda of Bhani, Punjab. I find my Panda in an ancient tenement, sitting on his wooden bed surrounded by folio volumes written in coarse hands. When I tell him my village and my name, he opens the proper volume to my genealogy and begins reading the history of my family: Mehta, Ved Parkash, son of Amolak Ram, son of Bhola Ram, son of Gian Chand, son of Karm Chand, son of Ram Jas Mal, son of Mansa Ram, son of Budhwant Rai. Amolak Ram, from his wife, Shanti Devi, daughter of Durga Das, begot seven children: Promila Kumari, Nirmal Kumari, Urmil Kumari, Om Parkash, Ved Parkash, Usha Kumari, Ashok Kumar. Bhola Ram, from his wife . . . The Panda runs over our birth dates, names, generations. For half an hour, he recites name after name after name. I stop him when he reads of my grandfather Bhola Ram's coming to Hardwar with the ashes of his father.

"That's nonsense," I say. "He lived more than two hundred miles from here, and he would have had to travel for days on foot and horesback, in bullock carts, tamtams, and trains. He could not have left the village for that long." And yet in the Panda's book the hand is unmistakably my grandfather's.

The Panda explains, "Remember what they were doing. They were depositing the ashes of their loved ones in the blessed Ganges. No hazard was too much, no journey was too long."

I get a copy of the genealogies for my mother. The Panda records my pilgrimage in his book. I give him a thank offering, and as I leave he says, "Now you must lead a new life." I'm off with his injunction to clean my slate. I wear my new suit of clothes, and, with no family to caution me, return home in a third-class compartment—part of Gandhi's India.

All through my journeys among the politicians and bureaus and through the villages where mud huts pass for homes, a bit of an acre passes for a farm, a hand plow passes for a tractor, a money-lender and a blacksmith pass for progress, naked, unhealthy bodies pass for human beings, ruins of a temple pass for the spiritual life, a handful of rice or corn passes for a meal from the beneficent God, one memory shines—Sunday lunch with Prime Minister Nehru.

At lunch, the Prime Minister eats with his hands, but he gives his guest a fork. I sit on his right, and his daughter, Mrs. Indira

Gandhi, is to my right. Two quiet grandsons in their teens make up the rest of the party. Mrs. Gandhi calls the Prime Minister "Papu," which seems to be a mixture of "Papa" and "Bapu." All of a sudden I feel that Gandhi, the Bapu of India, is there and the light hasn't gone out.

With his Gandhi cap on, the Prime Minister does not look old, but when he takes it off he looks his age. He has spent the morning at a hospital getting himself thoroughly checked by the doctors, and they say he will live for at least fifteen years more. He admits he has led a very strenuous life—long separation from family and friends, nine years in British prisons, unbroken periods of lonely counsel. He was left alone to guide India in its glory by the unseasonable death of Mahatma Gandhi. His aristocratic birth, his agnosticism, his faith in science and industrial society stood between him and Gandhi, but the man who shot the Mahatma for trying to quell the Hindu fury against the Muslims misunderstood the bond between Jawaharlal, the disciple, and Gandhi, the guru. A bullet could not touch Gandhi's spirit. At his death, the entire nation mourned for weeks. I remembered weeping as I listened to Nehru's tragic speech: "The light has gone out of our lives." Once the Bapu's triumphant spirit seemed to be no more, India's future was precarious, and the Prime Minister modestly acknowledges his contribution to her survival. Had he not withstood the shock of Gandhi's death, India might have been robbed forever of the light of independence.

While the bearer is crowding the brass plates with half a dozen little cups containing rice, vegetables, curry, and condiments, I'm struck by something that has existed throughout my visit with the Prime Minister but that I have just now recognized. His presence is nobly Indian. His features are pure Brahman; his buttoned-up coat and tight pajamas seem Moghul. When he speaks Hindi, it radiates ancient beauty; when he speaks English, he has the regal air of a king at a durbar. Speaking to an Oxford graduate of twenty-five, he shows a youthful sense of companionship that takes me by surprise. His intellectual grasp appears Indian and Western, ancient and modern. I recognize him. I feel I am confronting Sanskrit, Moghul, and English India at one time; he expresses the three Indias with their extremes but without their contradictions. His face suggests harmony, clarity, the quintessence of beauty.

Mrs. Gandhi, who is the official hostess for the Prime Minister, is the first woman of India. But her prëminence is hidden beneath the delicate charm with which she graces the luncheon. She prefers listening to the Prime Minister to talking herself. As a child, I was forced to eat yoghurt, and grew to regard it as an important issue dividing families and men, but now, having failed to eat rice and curry with my hands gracefully, I quickly gulp the yoghurt Mrs. Gandhi serves me. I apologize to the Prime Minister for turning a family lunch into a serious question period. He smiles. There are long silences between questions and answers, and these silences, which in any other circumstances would be nerve-racking, in his presence are restful.

While talking, we touch on the unfortunate division of India among religions, races, castes, and language groups, and the Prime Minister points to the troubled history that entangles modern India. Despite the divisions, he says, India manages to survive and go forward. In part, its progress is a compliment to the history of British administration, British law and order, but the compliment is soured by the conscious or unconscious policy of division that sometimes accompanied British administration; besides, law and order are conventions that often gloss over, rather than honestly meet and resolve, differences.

Again I feel that the real secret of one free India lies in the Prime Minister. His character reconciles the various Indias. The battle will come after his death, when the main combatants will knock each other to the ground, leaving the horses to dart about willy-nilly.

When Nehru is tired, he lies down and puts himself to sleep by reading. Last night, he says, he was reading a lecture that C. P. Snow recently delivered in Cambridge. Having been at one time a scientist, Nehru feels, with Snow, the dangers of increasing specialization—one of the more serious problems of modern society. He is never too busy to read, and tries to keep up with contemporary thought. His reading includes everything from poetry to zoology. He is not sure how many leaders have time to read, but he modestly maintains that there must be quite a few.

After lunch, we go into the sitting room. Mrs. Gandhi has the air-conditioner turned off, because "Papu" finds the room too cool. "The air-conditioner," she says, "is more for the benefit of the guests than of Papu." He has learned to live with the heat. I think I should leave, but the Prime Minister is relaxed and would love to talk. He reminisces about his Cambridge days. He doesn't know why he hasn't written much about Cambridge in his autobiographies. He was a solitary boy in England. "But," he adds, "those ancient universities are really good. They leave a lasting influence." It is a mistake when Oxford and Cambridge men try to re-create their universities in India. One cannot even go back to the university exactly as one left it. On returning to the universities, many of the graduates are disappointed. Fun at the university is part of adolescence, and adolescence cannot be recovered—at least, not by those who feel a social calling. And there is so much need for social feeling and responsibility. India is a good example of what remains to be done in the world. The developed societies seem to have reached their peaks, and sometimes they feel uncertain and frustrated with their wealth. But in India the frustration is of a different sort. It comes of too much to do instead of too little.

The Prime Minister admits that the Indians have not always obeyed the calling. In Sanskrit, for example, the literature to be discovered, annotated, and analysed is endless. Yet the Germans were the first to deal with our literature in a scientific and scholarly way. They gave a lead in this which was followed by Indian scholars. Sitting beside him and being talked to, as hundreds of young people must have been talked to by Gandhi, I can fathom the bond, the relationship, that must exist between a disciple and a guru. The simple sophistication of the Prime Minister leads me to wonder about the great Oxford figures who delighted in pretensions and eccentricities. They represented a nonconformist spirit continually trying to break through prescribed modes. The spirit was always searching to distinguish itself from the drab, the usual, the banal. And when the non-conformists, in their enthusiasm, sometimes exceeded the bounds, the academic community forgave the excesses because it commended the nonconformist spirit. As a result of my English education, I was prepared to meet some condescension from a great man, and, in an unrestrained moment, I tell the Prime Minister how surprised I am at being able to speak to him naturally.

This turns our conversation to England. The Prime Minister thinks England is still the most conservative country of Europe, and, despite the great social revolution since the Second World War, is still quite class-conscious. History spared England a sweeping revolution, and this tended to entrench her in her preserved prejudices; we, coming as we do from a caste-ridden society, are in a good position to appreciate both the advantages and the disadvantages of a conservative society. With a youthful smile, he admits that if an Indian is blessed with social graces and educated in the ways of English society he can be very happy in England. Indeed, the Prime Minister is quite aware that some Indians, even today, prefer the certainties of the dead British raj to the uncertainties of freedom. He agrees that the choice between authority and freedom is not just Indian but is as old as history. It is, in another form, the choice between being a contented animal and being Socrates. But, he adds with compassion, we must not judge harshly. "We are children of habit, and habit is not easily changed," he says. He agrees that we are torn in our loyalties between British India and our own, the first with established standards, the second at present lacking standards. In British India, we race with a handicap, because all that we can do is often done better by Englishmen. Indian India is naturally our own, but it will be a long time before we can reach a Western degree of advancement. Meanwhile, we are condemned to fall between the two worlds and tolerate an existence more superficial than satisfactory.

He questions me about my education, my interests, and what I should like to do in life. He recommends a career of writing, and refers to India's need for more writers, painters, sculptors, musicians, and dancers. "But," he adds candidly, "while India needs people like you, I'm not sure she can at present really afford them." India, he explains, has so many fundamental needs to fill that he doesn't know when we will get beyond them and be able to subsidize culture, as we would like to, in a major way. He feels, however, that difficulties can be stimulating, and points to our many distinguished creative and scholarly works. Worthwhile men, he says, never shrink from hazards and hardships. I am left feeling that the problems we are facing are of epic proportions, and that men who wish to do their duty must measure up to the heroic possibilities. While heroism seems to be playing out in the West, it is just beginning in the East.

Nehru, for one, doesn't appear to be sitting on the issues. He walks and talks, moving from subject to subject with ease. It seems that his India is going through its gestation period and may be longer at it than our cherished elephants. The Prime Minister prays for peace. He hopes that the new India will be given a chance to show her mettle. He prays that we will not be stunted in our growth. He hopes for better times than we have known so far in our century. In this he is no different from anyone else, he adds, but when many are paralysed by depression, it is left to the thinking and pioneering men to break fresh ground. He says that his work is not always intellectually engaging, and thanks me for talking with him. I am left aghast, and wonder how the Prime Minister of India can spare time for private individuals.

His parting words to me are "Come and talk to me whenever the spirit moves you."

"I wouldn't know the protocol," I say.

"Just ring up my secretary," he says. "It is as easy as that."

I come away feeling that Nehru is as great as Gandhi, and that it is circumstance that has prevented him from shaping younger leaders. It is easy for Prasads to yield their lives for a movement, but it is much more difficult for young Prasads to commit themselves to the thankless day-by-day routine of building a nation with bricks and mortar. I remember hearing Dom Moraes say after an interview with the Prime Minister that

Nehru was doing with India what poets do with words. I come away from the Prime Minister feeling that in India there is promise. I'm learning to walk the Indian streets.

Once more, I am in a plane. I am returning to the West, but this time my journey has direction. I am not shifting from plane to plane, from taxi to taxi, as in the bummy days. I must complete my Western education before I settle in India.

I open my journal and begin thumbing through my impressions of the summer in India. My journey is like my own life—humdrum, disjointed, and untidy. It does not have dates. I lean on my journal as a record of revealing moments—the photographs of happenings as I focused on them at the time.

I turn my attention from the journal to what is outside. There is not much there. The Indian land mass is obscured beneath leaden clouds. The clouds are dense, but they are not the frightening thunderheads of the monsoons. The jet rides like a large bus wheeling its way through snow, but without skids and jerks. This Comet is not at all like the DC-3 that took me to Nepal or like the Viscount that carried me away from Calcutta; its motor has the even hum of a smooth and powerful machine, and after a while, like a factory worker, I become accustomed to the noise.

I nod to the hostess, who is quite charming. She talks of inconsequentials—the weather, the distance to Karachi.

I return to the journal.

Page 200. Today, received letter from great friend at Balliol, Jasper Griffin. Takes exception to my letter about days with Dom : " What is this awful word ' bummy ' with which you make so free? I never heard it from you—or, indeed, from anyone—in Oxford. Nor were you really as dissolute and irresponsible as you try to make out; though you won't thank me for reminding you of the fact, you were actually a pillar of respectability and straight living—even to your daily dark suit. You were even abstemious with drink. You are an old fraud, and I have a mind to denounce you to the public as the moral man you are." But writers, like cats, must live several lives. Life is bundle of little truths; art is a way to greater truth.

I look for my last meeting with the Prime Minister.

Page 202. Today I met him again. Really a man of many faces. Not only Brahman, regal, English, but ingenious politician, saint, good theoretician. "If you feel you must go, you must. Your project is worthwhile. You are right to follow your interests and go in search of your documents. You will not turn your back on the problems and the country. There are all kinds of activity. If I had not been drawn into politics, I would have taken up writing. Not fiction—I lack that sort of imagination." (Dom : Doing with India what poets do with words.) Very understanding, mysterious ability to fix people in a fraction of a moment and see the whole.

The hostess comes up and serves me coffee. "The weather is not bad," she says. "We will soon be clear of it." The land is still veiled in clouds. They have thinned out a bit, exposing the jungles under the haze.

It is difficult to find anything in my journal, and the jungle of impressions and disconnected experiences makes bad reading. The summer in India is blurred and misty.

We are flying over the Indian Ocean, and there isn't a single cloud; it is beautifully clear. I have slept on my impressions, and feel refreshed. The hostess brings me some paper, and I begin to make notes on my journal, rearranging facts and days, trying to give it all some order and shape.